Beat the Fraudster

How to Easily Protect Yourself Online and Offline

Doug McAdam

Interior and Cover Designer: Laura Rimmer
Lead Editor: Laura Rimmer
Images: Doug McAdam
ISBN: 978-1-9196224-9-1

For more information and resources, please visit Doug's website at www.BeatTheFraudster.com.

Table of Contents

INTRODUCTION

CYBERCRIME IS NOW A BIGGER THREAT THAN PHYSICAL CRIME

What benefits do you accrue by reading this?

As the world constantly changes, more crime is being perpetrated through electronic means: 'cyber-crime'. I have shared ideas as to how to protect yourself better with friends and colleagues and it was suggested I share them with the wider public – hence this book.

The BBC reports that you are 10-times more likely to be a victim of some sort of fraud/cyber-crime than you are being burgled.

BIO

Having travelled extensively for personal reasons and serving a short stint with the armed forces, I developed a keen interest in protecting myself from threats, to the extent I have created useful tactics to better protect myself and my family. By sharing these with you, I hope you can implement some to better protect you and your family.

The protocols expanded upon are derived through experimentation. This has served as motivation to create better protocols to further protect myself and family in the future. For better context, over the last 10 years, the following events have occurred:

1. My credit cards have been cloned on several occasions. People who travel for business report they receive 3-4 fraud attempts each year.
    a. Many attempts were picked up by the automated fraud system contained within the banking system, resulting in one of those automated bank calls, asking you to verify some transactions.
2. My PayPal account was hacked
3. My eBay account was hacked
4. My Netflix account was also hacked - the password repeatedly stopped working over a period of weeks, resulting in a constant password reset. Each time it was changed, it was hacked again. Netflix

was called and it was then discovered that the hackers had increased the permitted viewing devices in order for them to view Netflix for free. It was caught before the first increased payment was charged. Our Netflix account was closed and a new one created - *see domain names section later in the book.*

5. A bank account hacked and the fraudster obtained thousands. Having paid for a reputable anti-virus, the bank scanned my computer and was satisfied I did not have a *Keylogger* software, which facilitated an expedited refund by the bank. *Keylogger* software is malicious software that records all keystrokes including passwords. This usually is installed on your computer by clicking on a link within a spam email, or a fraudulent website you visited unwittingly. This is why the login process on some websites (e.g., banks) uses a section that requires a mouse to click a drop-down-menu. As far as I know, software cannot track mouse movements.

Most of the advice given in this handbook will be easy to follow. For more technical areas there is abundant help available - *any technical terminology will be explained.* While I consider myself an advanced computer user, I am not an expert. Some areas will require specialist help. Each relevant section will advise on where you can obtain free technical support, hence there is no need to rely on Google searches which often result in an information overload.

Complacency is your enemy. It only takes that one occasion when we: forget to lock a car door, the shed or back gate. The world is changing; why does the criminal bother stealing £50/$50 worth of equipment from your car or shed, when they can gain access to your network/phone/bank stealing thousands of your hard-earned money.

Because *stranger danger* it is drummed into our minds from a young age, most of us are aware of securing ourselves physically, but many of us like the convenience and ease phones and computers give us. The fraudster takes advantage of this using our desire for convenience against us, just like the opportunistic criminal looking for the unlocked car. This has migrated into even more sophisticated means as they look for the easy targets; e.g., not covering your PIN, not securing your home network, unlocked phones, etc.

Some of the procedures in this book are one-off events you initiate to make your virtual world safe; others are on-going, like remembering to lock the car or covering your PIN.

Chapter outline:

1. Real life scams that have occurred; some appear far-fetched, but have real victims.
2. How to spot fraudulent emails and texts with Tips and Traps.
3. Spotting
   a. The tell tail sign you are on a genuine banking website vs. fraudulent one.
   b. Real vs. fraudulent web address (known as URL).
   c. How to protect yourself.
4. How they make any number they choose (your bank) appear on your screen and how to determine if the call you are receiving is genuine or fake.
5. General advice on bank cards/entering your PIN/ATM's how you can reorganise your banking to restrict any damage and inconvenience to you.
6. Advice of when you should logout of your apps.
7. How to stay safe on public Wi-Fi and the use of VPN's.
8. Why they are important, tips on creating passwords and password managers.
9. Enhancing your home or work protection – Free help available from your internet provider.
10. How you can compartmentalise your life with a domain name (domain names are explained) – Free help available from domain companies.
11. If your PayPal is hacked, you don't want to lose your online purchase history, because it is your proof of purchase.
12. Using multiple email address to create multiple PayPal accounts.
13. How to use message rules and filters with your email provider – Free help available from your internet provider.
14. Bullet point reminder list.

DEFINITIONS

DEVICES – this is generic term used to describe any computer device including:

➢ Mobile phones/cell phones

- ➢ Tablets (iPads and Android), Phablet (cross between phone and tablet)
- ➢ Laptop computers
- ➢ Desktop computers
- ➢ On any operating system (OS), including:
  - ○ Windows
  - ○ MAC
  - ○ IOS (apple)
  - ○ Android
  - ○ Are the major ones

Whenever the word 'device(s)' is used throughout the book, assume I mean all of the above, because most scams can affect any type of device connected to the internet, including smart devices such as a smart TV or home heating.

VIGILANCE

During any crisis, the fraudster thinks of new and inventive ways to con you. Just as we had new scams following the Icelandic volcanic ash cloud that blew across Europe in 2011 which grounded most planes; the Covid-19 pandemic is no different.

- Scammers offering travel refunds; asking for your card details, whilst the real travel company already has them.
- Whenever something is going on in your life be it a pandemic, the loss of loved ones, or any other personal or national problem, we let our guards down and are more susceptible to believing the fraudster.

RELIANCE ON THE BANKING SECTOR

Where banks have closed branches in remote parts of the country, it has forced towns to become cashless, which increases its reliance on the electronic banking services. Therefore, if you are targeted and fall a victim, the effect is further compounded if you don't have a backup plan.

Following the advice in this book can mitigate damages suffered to reduce or avoid the resources spent fixing the problem, because it never happens at a convenient time. *The last two occasions I had my credit card cloned, I was at work whilst my wife was making the weekly grocery shopping, which was abruptly ended when the credit card got cancelled.*

WHAT HAPPENS WHEN THINGS GO WRONG

Should you fall victim, the fallout will be very stressful.

- ➢ You may lose sleep.
- ➢ Be easily irritable.
- ➢ In some rare cases people can manifest physical symptoms of stress.
- ➢ Fall into depression.

CONSEQUENCES

- ➢ At one end of the spectrum, we have a cloned card – the bank's antifraud system identifies a possible fraud, cancels your card, have a new one re-issued and catch up on outstanding payments.
  - o If the banks antifraud system, doesn't identify it, the last resort is to check your bank & credit card statements.
- ➢ At the other end of the spectrum where your identity is stolen and used to commit fraud as well as steal your money. The fallout includes:
  - o Bank accounts are closed.
  - o Fraud marker against your name which prevents you from opening new accounts.
  - o Cannot receive salary from your employer.
  - o Cannot pay important bills.
  - o Arrested and having to prove your innocence; being arrested can have lasting effects on some jobs, especially anyone working with children or in civil positions of authority e.g., military personnel.
  - o You could lose a job and by the time it is resolved, your employer has replaced you.
  - o It can take more than 12-months to resolve a stolen identity.

PREVENTION

Just as we wear seat belts to prevent injury, following this advice can prevent financial jeopardy. You don't have to implement all the procedures at once. You can review and implement over time.

- ➢ Some sections are a one-off task:
  - o Compartmentalising your banking in - chapter 5.
  - o Increasing security of your home network in - chapter 9.
- ➢ Other areas are on a continuous basis, such as how to be constantly vigilant to spot scams within text messages, emails and cloned websites.

STEP BY STEP

Often victims are defrauded in stages, many without knowing. Smaller scams can lead to you be a perpetual target. If you fall for smaller scam/fraud, they may see you as a candidate for further fraud.

1) If you become a victim of a scam, you can put on a 'suckers list' that criminals sell onto other criminals.

2) They will build up a picture of your life in stages, dates, pets, children, habits and use these details to impersonate you when calling the phone company to obtain a duplicate sim card so they can receive SMS codes sent by the bank, moving onto to bank fraud.

You never know who is trying to defraud you. Just as you lock your house or car whenever you exit because you do not know when someone will attempt to gain access whilst you are away. Therefore, we need to always be careful to protect digital information, because you will be unaware when they are unsuccessful and only aware they are successful.

Some areas may seem tedious while others will take a little time to implement. Review one section in detail each month so it is not overwhelming

➢ Opening new bank accounts to compartmentalise and ring-fence your finances – it will take time to open bank accounts and switch direct debits & standing orders.

➢ Talking to your internet service provider for assistance to improve security, how to set up 'guest Wi-Fi' and change default passwords.

1. GENERAL SECURITY TIPS AND POPULAR SCAMS

1.1. PERMITTED ACCESS

On occasions we have to allow technical support or people in a position of authority to log into a sensitive area, such as remote computer access, send a computer away for repair, website administration, remote support for software or general assistance.

Obviously, the best practice would be to initially change your password to a temporary one until the issue is resolved, after which you can return the password to any of your choosing.

Example 1: You send your computer for repairs. You change the password to something else, e.g., '1234' and upon its return change the password back. Of course, if you are unable to create a temporary password, don't reuse the previous password upon its return.

Example 2. You are experiencing some technical issues and then you give your admin login to your tech support in order for them to resolve the issue. If you cannot create a temporary password, ensure you change it once the issue is resolved.

NOTE: some online accounts don't permit the repeated use of previous passwords, meaning if you change your password to a temporary one, you <u>will not</u> be able to restore the previous password; eBay has this protocol.

<u>CASE STUDY TRUE STORY</u>: *'John' used a technical support person to assist with his website, completely forgetting this technical support still had access. Approximately one year later, the tech support then used John's credentials to gain access to his website altering his pricing and other items, causing John to lose business.*

For the most part, tech support individuals are very trustworthy and will never use any sensitive information maliciously, but it only takes that one.

<u>GOLDEN RULES</u>**:**
- ➤ If you permit access to an online service or account, change the password once access is no longer required.
- ➤ If an employee within your company that had access to a Wi-Fi, computer, payroll, accounts, suppliers ordering, or literally anything leaves the company, change the password or, revoke their privileges.
- ➤ Ex-employees have been known to use their credentials for malicious purposes. If you use a cloud-based bookkeeping package and decide to change bookkeepers or accountants, you should remove their access.
    - ○ From 2018 the UK had instituted stiff data protection laws. If a disgruntled employee uses your Wi-Fi for malicious purposes, or sells that code to a criminal and you lose personal data of staff/customers, you can and will be fined thousands of pounds/dollars. It only takes five minutes to change computer and Wi-Fi codes.
- ➤ If you hand over your phone to be repaired, change the passcode first to a temporary one.

1.2. MOBILE PHONE -1

When the fraudster thinks they have enough information to impersonate you with your bank, or over the phone; the first step is they contact your phone supplier to obtain a new SIM card so they can intercept any OTP (One-time Passcodes).

WARNING: If your mobile phone coverage *'goes dark'* (sudden loss of signal) for no apparent reason while other family members using the same network remain unaffected, there is a reasonable chance you are under attack. <u>CONTACT YOUR BANK IMMEDIATELY</u>. The fraudster will be looking to either obtain a loan in your name or transfer money directly from your account. The bank should set up a new password, or put a temporary freeze on your account to help prevent it. A quick response is key. The reason your phone went dark is because the fraudster has already obtained a replacement SIM card from your phone provider and has just activated the SIM card so they may receive the OTP (one-time passcodes) when setting up new payments and applications.

1.3. MOBILE PHONE -2

Whilst dining out, it's recommended not to place your phone on the table. Be sure to place it in your pocket or bag, as it is too easy for phones to be stolen from a table, especially when seated outside. It only takes your attention to be divided for half a second; bear in mind that criminals work in groups and it is most likely the conspirator that is causing the distraction to divert your attention.

CASE STUDY: *'Lorraine' and 'Barbara' are sitting outdoors at a café drinking coffee in Barcelona. A gypsy approaches asking for money but does this by placing a note written in English over the top of Lorraine's mobile phone which was left on the table. Neither woman notice the gypsy swipe the phone from under the notice and pass it onto her younger sister standing next to her, looking equally as sad. It's a surprisingly common occurrence, especially in Mediterranean countries.*

Not to mention, if you have to evacuate quickly for any reason, you will need your phone to get help, family or the authorities and you do not want to leave it behind in the mad rush.

1.4. DRIVING LICENCE – CASE STUDY

CASE STUDY TRUE STORY: *'Kostas' was pulled over by the police and made to sit in the back of the police car. When his driving licence was returned by the police officer, it was not secured properly in his wallet and so it fell out on the back seat of the police car. Later found by the officer, the officer proceeded to return it. As there was no response at the mailing address, the officer posted it through the letterbox. 'Kostas' had in fact moved but not updated his address. The new occupant of the property used the driving licence to commit identity fraud, naturally causing great distress and financial problems for 'Kostas' while taking a lot of time to resolve.*

If you ever lose your Licence, the finder could steal your identity, sell your details or even just return it to the wrong address. Having the wrong address means they can do more damage before you discover it making it harder, longer and more costly to resolve. Having your correct address will make it harder for criminals; as well as giving you a better chance of it being returned to you safely.

1.5. PICKPOCKETS AND MUGGINGS

➢ It goes without saying that you should never keep anything in your trouser back pockets. Too many men keep their wallets there and many young women keep their phones there with it often slightly protruding. If you need proof, take a look at YouTube where you will see this in action; pick pockets on skateboards, bicycles or mopeds helping themselves because they have speed on their side, with you having no chance to recover your belongings.

➢ When travelling I carry: a small plastic wallet, the type that is big enough for two cards only. On one side I insert an out-of-date credit card, on the other I have approx. £20/$20 worth of local currency. If I am pickpocketed they will hopefully be satisfied enough not to come back; if you are confronted and mugged you can let them go, whilst you disappear into a crowd.

    ○ Do not use a debit card as they also contain your banking sort code and account number, unless it is a debit card to an account that no longer exists, i.e., a closed account.

    ○ If you have ever experienced credit card fraud, where your card is subsequently cancelled and you were re-issued a new card, don't destroy your old card; you now have a non-working card with what appears as a valid expiration date. This is better than an out-of-date card because, at first glance to the criminal, it will appear to be a valid card. There is no exposure to the card company because the card has already been cancelled.

➢ If you hear in a public place on a Public Address (PA) system "be-careful, there are pickpockets working in this area", the natural thing is to pat yourself where your wallet or purse is located. Unfortunately, you have now just shown all the thieves watching the area where your wallet/purse is located. Better to check it a minute later, pop into a toilet or find a discrete area, perhaps with your back is to the wall.

➢ As mentioned in 1.3, when sitting down at a cafe, never place your phone on the table. It only takes a second's distraction for it to be stolen. This is actually more common than pickpockets.

➢ Never hang your bag on the back of your chair; it's out of sight. Better to place put your leg or a chair leg through one of the straps. A small bag can be placed on the table in full view at all times.

- ➢ If you hang a jacket on the back of your chair, do not leave anything of value in any pocket.
- ➢ Recap:
    - o Keep pockets and bags zipped up.
    - o Do not leave valuables in jackets/coats on the back of a chair.
    - o Do not hang a bag on the back of a chair.
    - o Do put your leg or a chair leg through your bag handle, so it cannot be swiped when you are distracted.
- ➢ At home it is too easy to become complacent and you should use these tactics whether at home or overseas.

When travelling locally or further afield disguise where your valuables are located on you. There are some great items of clothing with many hidden pockets available on the market including: scarfs, T-shirts, leggings, underwear. A couple of favourite sites are:
https://www.clevertravelcompanion.com/ & https://www.scottevest.com/

1.6. HOTELS
1.6.1. ROOM KEY (SWIPE KIND)
It has been reported that your magnetic room key holds a lot more data than just your room number. In some cases, it can hold all your billing details such as: Full name, address & credit card details.

Have you ever noticed when you check out your room, keys are just dumped in a basket at Reception until reused, especially if you use the self-checkout by using the slot in the counter to a basket underneath?

Have you also noticed they are coded for the next person upon arrival? There is a potential gold mine of sellable information - YOUR INFORMATION - just lying around to be taken by a rogue employee or criminal.

TIP: When travelling, carry a small magnet and when exiting the room for the LAST TIME, swipe the magnetic strip on the hotel card with your magnet. Attempt to re-enter your room to ensure the card is wiped. If you do not have a magnet, buy a cheap small fridge magnet from any of tourist vendor. You can even discard your new magnet in the hotel lobby if you don't want to take it home.

1.6.2. HOTEL DOOR HANDLE CARD

When you exit your room for the day, you may well have used the door handle card saying "PLEASE CLEAN MY ROOM".

1. It won't get the maid to your room any quicker; they operate a predefined sequence for efficiency.
2. This tells any rogue employee with a master key you are out. In some parts of the world, some staff seek out such rooms. Please remember in poorer countries - maids, waiters etc. often earn as little as a few hundred pounds/dollars per month for a full-time job.

1.6.3. PASSPORT

1. When you receive your passport back from a hotel employee, ensure it is yours – even an employee who is distracted by a phone call can make a genuine mistake.
2. When you reapply and receive your new passport in your home country – double check the details. I experienced an incorrect DOB on my passport and it was not noticed until at the airport check-in desk. Fortunately, I was still permitted to fly with instructions to rectify it immediately upon return, but you may not be so lucky.

1.7 SOCIAL MEDIA SCAM INCLUDING TEXT MESSAGE and MESSAGE APPS SUCH AS WHATSAPP

Fraudsters will hack people's social media accounts and wait for an appropriate time to pounce. The same can apply though text messages including messaging platforms such as WhatsApp.

HOW IT WORKS: The fraudsters will message a friend asking for a small loan to pay bills e.g., £300/$300 as an emergency, or even your employer/supervisor asking you to buy a number of vouchers e.g., Amazon vouchers 5x £100/$100. In all cases you are put under pressure.

It is fine to help your friends, family or work colleagues in times of need, but verify the request and their bank details via another method such as text or email, even better, call them.

1.8. ROMANCE FRAUD

Many people are shy when it comes to romance, which is why so many find comfort and ease with finding romance online and/or through social media. If someone you have not met personally asks you for money, especially in the thousands, you'd obviously say NO! Romance Fraud is another fraudulent area which is growing rapidly.

The warning signs are:

> ➢ Sob story – some sort of traumatic event, injury, or being stranded. It will be a desperate plight.
> ➢ You make arrangements – particularly to meet, but they are cancelled last minute; e.g., job interview, family emergency, usually something you don't feel you can question.
> ➢ Some sort of financial request, it may be very small at the on-set.
> ➢ Boasts of income, wealth, status e.g., "family in the state department", move around a lot.
> ➢ They become defensive if challenged.

Many people have lost tens of thousands. Official crime statistics feel the true losses are much higher due to people not reporting it, because they are embarrassed they have been conned this way. DON'T BE! it is not your fault. Knowledge is power and your knowledge shared may just prevent others from falling victim.

Remember these criminals play on your heartstrings and loneliness; they often spend many months cultivating and grooming relationships as a full-time job.

A romance fraud survivor has written a book on her experience – Jan Marshall 'Romance scam survivor'. Available on Amazon.

WHAT CAN YOU DO?

If you are courting online:

> ✓ Search other sites for the same person to see if they are communicating with other people.
> ✓ Google and use other social media such as Facebook search to see if you can find other photos to compare.
> ✓ Fact check – do what you can to double check their facts.
> ✓ Don't be afraid to offend by asking straightforward questions.
> ✓ Meet as soon as possible.

- ✓ Share details with your friends as this offers a fresh perspective.
- ✓ Go slow and beware of premature love declarations, or requests for sexy photos.
- ✓ Pick holes, repeat questions over several chats, ask the same question a different way. If they are a fraudster, they are likely to be chatting to many people during the course of the day, they will forget who they have told what.
- ✓ Search online "REVERSE IMAGE LOOKUP", you can upload photos and the website will search billions of online photos to see if they have been used before.
- ✓ Watch the BBC scam program 'FOR LOVE OR MONEY' available on the 'BBC iPlayer'.

1.9 MONEY MULE

You may have heard of a *'drug mule'* (someone who carries drugs when travelling); well, a *'money mule'* is something different. A money mule is someone who unwittingly allows a criminal to launder their money through your bank account. Criminals actively target young people through social media, with a promise of earning quick stress-free cash without doing any work, often making hundreds of pounds in a matter of minutes.

Young people are targeted because their bank accounts are likely to be clean with little history. By using individuals without a criminal or banking history, it is harder for the authorities to trace and follow the money.

HOW IT WORKS: Criminals use law-abiding citizens with genuine bank accounts to launder their money. The money is paid into your bank account (usually in cash), with instructions for you (the 'mule'), to transfer the money onto other bank accounts after deducting your agreed fee. The money then appears to be clean because it is coming from an account belonging to a law-abiding citizen.

A popular ruse is "earn money from home".

HOW YOU ARE CAUGHT: All banks look out for similar transactions and the bank may freeze your account.

WHAT HAPPENS IF YOU ARE CAUGHT: The fact is this is money laundering which is illegal. The money you forward on, will be used to fund further criminal activities such as drug and/or people trafficking or terrorism. The repercussions you can face are:

- ➤ Your bank account and other bank accounts frozen.
- ➤ All your money seized as well as the criminal's money.
- ➤ Your bank account shut down.
- ➤ Difficulty in opening new bank accounts – this is because anyone who has a bank account closed by the bank is placed on an anti-fraud watch list.
- ➤ Difficulty in obtaining loans, credit cards and mortgages or even problems passing credit check for new rental accommodation.
- ➤ A very likely criminal prosecution and possible custodial sentence.
- ➤ You may feel the effect for several years.

HOW TO STOP: If you have become a victim, it would be impossible to stop anyone from depositing money into your account, I suggest the following:

- ➤ Don't respond to any more social media conversation.
- ➤ Report the social media account as suspicious and explain they are attempting to lure you in.
- ➤ Don't spend the money, you could face physical threat of violence.
- ➤ You could inform your bank, but be warned they may feel they have to report you to the authorities.
- ➤ You could inform the police.
- ➤ If you fear reprisals from the authorities, move only your money to another bank account, switching any direct debits/standing orders to that new account and close the original bank account. The criminals cannot pay money into a closed bank account.

REMEMBER:

- ➤ If it sounds to be good to be true, it usually is.
- ➤ Take a step back, to consider.
- ➤ Discuss it with a friend or family member; you can also consult your solicitor or accountant if you have one.
- ➤ You won't lose money by not taking part.
- ➤ Don't give out your bank details to anyone you don't know and trust.

1.10 SOCIAL MEDIA

Fraudsters can gather many personal details about individuals, from social media such as pets, birthdays etc.

I have seen some dangerous things on social media:

> Photo of a driving licence – this is perfect for identity theft.
> Individuals posting a countdown to their holiday; This highlights the exact dates your property will be empty. Even if you have a house sitter, they do not know that, you do not want uninvited visitors.

An experiment was conducted during a documentary where a presenter, acting as a psychic, was fed information via an ear piece while a team behind the screen was going through social media for personal information as mentioned above. The team was revealed afterwards, demonstrating how they had managed to gather such information. This is proof of how easy it is to obtain your personal information via social media. **You can view yourself; search on YouTube "amazing mind reader reveals his 'gift'".**

TIP: Most Romance Fraudsters (SCAM 1.8) steel your unprotected images from your social media accounts, steeling your identity. This is demonstrated on the BBC scam program 'FOR LOVE OR MONEY' available on the *'BBC iPlayer'*; ensure you check your privacy settings and do not leave your social media account open.

1.11 TILL SCAMS

A new scam emerged in 2019 and appears to be global issue. Checkout staff often now ask if you want a receipt (maybe to help save the planet by not printing one), but this opened up an opportunity for dishonest employees.

It is perpetrated upon on low value transactions such as the type where the PIN is not requested (known as contactless/pay-wave/express-pay and perhaps other names in other countries).

HOW IT WORKS: Many retailers permit *'cash-back'* which is where you add a small amount to your transaction total and the employee hands you the extra cash as charged. In essence, the till is an alternative for an ATM. In the UK *cash-back* is usually limited to £50.

The rogue employee will add a small amount such as £10/$20 to the bill in the hope that you don't check the amount on the POS terminal. The cash will simply be handed off to an accomplice as their change, who is probably somewhere behind you in the queue, meaning it will never be spotted on CCTV. Regular customers who routinely say no to a receipt are targeted as they are remembered as not taking a receipt.

PREVENTION:
1. Always check the amount on the PIN terminal before waving your card, or entering your PIN.
2. Always ask for receipt, even if you dispose of it outside, or recycle it at home.
3. Check your receipt for *cash-back*.

OTHER REASONS FOR OBTAINING A RECEIPT:
1. You realise you forgot something and return to the shop still holding the items just purchased.
2. The items just bought are out of date/rotten/damaged.
3. You realise you bought the wrong item and want to exchange it.

1.12 OVERPAYMENT SCAM
In the UK, back in the good old days there was a thing called *'cheque guarantees'*, when you presented your cheque (check to our U.S. readers) with the debit cards to the same account, you could guarantee a cheque up to the level on the back of your card. This usually ranged from £50-£250. Once done, the retailer would know the money is guaranteed, as the purchaser could not stop it.

This system ceased in 2011. Since then, a cheque is never safe even after the cheque has cleared and the funds are in your account. If the originating bank discovers the cheque is fraudulent or stolen, they will make a charge-back against the recipient; this means that you have the money taken off you even when cleared. There is also no time limit, so this can occur many months after you received the funds.

HOW IT WORKS: You are selling some personal items on second hand platform e.g., Gumtree, Facebook market place, local paper etc. where a buyer offers to pay by cheque. They give some rouse about a work cheque budget they are allowed to spend offering you 2-3 times the asking price asking that you refund the difference in cash or to another bank account. Once the cheque has cleared and you have refunded the overpayment, the cheque is reported as stolen or the bank discovers fraudulent activity, perhaps the cheque belongs to a victim so the bank charges you to recover the money from your account.

It isn't really a business/work cheque. That is just a rouse to reel you in. In reality it will be either the fraudster's own cheque so they report it stolen and get their money back or the fraudster has stolen a cheque book resulting in two victims, you and the owner of the stolen cheque book.

CASE STUDY: *You are selling a piece of furniture for £200/$200. The buyer says, "My employer is buying this and I am permitted to spend £600/$600, can I give you a cheque for £600/$600 and once it is cleared, you refund me the balance of £400/$400". In reality you are* <u>unaware</u> *the fraudster has stolen the cheque book. You agree to the transaction and duly refund £400/$400 in a week's time. Sometime after this, the victim of the stolen cheque book reports the fraud to their bank which in turn contacts your bank to flag it as a fraudulent transaction, so your bank automatically debits your account by £600/$600 (the value of the cheque) refunding to the victim of the stolen cheque book. The result being that you have now lost £1000/$1000 (the £400/$400 refund plus £600/$600 chargeback) and the goods you were selling. In some cases, they don't bother collecting the items you sold.*

GOLDEN RULE: Do not accept overpayments and do not accept cheques. If you cannot meet the buyer, accepting payments through PayPal is a much safer method of payment.

1.13 COURIER FRAUD
It starts by receiving all call where they state they are calling from the police or fraud department of your bank. The scam does work better on a landline for reason that will become clear.

HOW IT WORKS: In the case of the police impersonation, they may ask you to call 999/911/112 (emergency services) and explain to the operator it is not an emergency but you are calling to verify the identity of police officer on the phone.

In either case of a police officer or a member of staff from the bank fraud team:

18

- They may ask lots of questions about which cards you have or which banks you have accounts with.
- They will then tell a story about gangs and how they suspect staff members involvement and ask for your assistance to catch them.
- They will want you to go to the bank to draw out cash, or may say your account has been frozen.
- At some point they will transfer the call to your mobile.
- They will ask you to keep your phone ON in your pocket at all times, so they can listen.
- They will ask if you can withdraw the funds.
- They will ask you to hand the cash to a motor cycle courier or police officer who won't remove their helmet.
- The courier may be a genuine courier paid for the job to create distance with the fraudster.
- If you cannot get to the bank quickly, they will pay for a taxi to pick you and take you home.
- They will tell you that the police will return your money in person with lots of forms to complete.

You will never see your money again and to add insult to injury, you will have to pay for the cab fare.

TIP: The police will never ask a member of the public to assist in an investigation; they cannot guarantee your safety. Nor would they ask to use your own money as bait.

TIP: Remember, that in the UK when a landline calls another landline and the recipient replaces the handset, <u>the call is not disconnected</u>, fraudsters will play a tune down the phone, mimicking a dial tone, so when you pick it up again, you think you are making a fresh call, <u>but a conspirator will act as the emergency services operator</u> and put you back to the 'police officer', which is not a police officer.

1.14 TRADESMAN SCAM WITH YOUR Wi-Fi.
<u>CASE STUDY TRUE STORY</u>: *Ann is house-sitting for her friend Bella when a tradesman arrives to check the drains and appears to know Bella and that she may be away. Ann thinks Bella forgot to mention that someone was coming, so let's him in. What we don't know is Bella's children has friends that always*

come around and use the Wi-Fi. Bella has her Wi-Fi code written on a chalk board. The tradesman uses the ruse to scan the premises but is searching for the Wi-Fi code, once found he proceeds to check the drains. Once he completes his (pretend) inspection, he says, "I am popping to the van to see if I have a part and if not, I will order one". He sits in the van appearing to be on the phone. After five minutes, he drives off never to be seen again. A few weeks later Bella is the victim of severe bank fraud losing thousands.

What was actually happening when he went to the van, he was actually gaining access to the Wi-Fi and possibly installing 'spyware' on all computers/laptops/tablets etc.' SPYWARE' is software that allows criminals to watch and record your activity. In the following weeks he sat outside accessing the Wi-Fi, using his spyware, waiting and watching for Bella to access all her bank accounts and credit card details online; once he has enough information on Bella, he uses her details to access all her accounts and steals all her money.

Don't have your Wi-Fi code displayed.

A better solution is to use the 'guest network' feature on your router. Guest networks have restrictions. Please see chapter 9, section 5 (Para 9.5) the guest Wi-Fi feature is very good to protect your privacy.

Also, to prevent someone from using your Wi-Fi (or at least makes it harder for the fraudster to gain access), is to enable 'MAC ADDRESS FILTERING'. Please see chapter 9 section 8 (Para 9.8) where MAC ADDRESS FILTERING is explained in detail.

1.15 PERFUME SCAM
CASE STUDY TRUE STORY: Paige was walking to her car in a supermarket car park when a couple approaches and asked, "What kind of perfume do you wear?", slightly confused, she asked, "Why?" They said "We are selling some name brand perfumes, at reasonable prices. Would I like to sample some fabulous scents?" Paige replied, "I have no money". He then pulled from his pocket a perfume strip with a perfume on it. Paige looked quickly at it and gave it back repeating "I have no money" He said, "It is OK, we take cheque or credit cards". Being scared, so just got in the car and said "no thanks".

THIS IS NOT PERFUME...IT IS ETHER! When you sniff it, you will pass out.

You will be robbed and heaven knows what else.

1.16 MANDATE FRAUD
Emails are often hacked but the fraudster will not take immediate action, they will watch and wait for an opportunity to target you. When emails are hacked the fraudster can:
- ➢ Intercept emails before they reach the recipient.
- ➢ Change bank details.
- ➢ Open attachments to amend details, then re-attach the document e.g., PDF invoice.
- ➢ Release the email on its way.

CASE STUDY TRUE STORY-1: (Reported on BBC Radio4 in 2019)
Carol was having an extension built (we will ignore the reason why she was paying so much money in one go. That is another matter; don't pay in advance, pay as each stage is completed). The builder emailed over the invoice for payment as a PDF document attached to the email for £60,000 with a note on the email "please note my new bank details". Carol transferred the £60,000. A week later, the builder followed up with Carol for the payment and Carol said, "I have paid you on the new bank details" to which the builder replied; "I don't have any new bank details"; and the penny drops.

CASE STUDY TRUE STORY-2: (Reported on BBC Radio4 in 2020)
Elizabeth and her partner, were buying a house and it came time to transfer their deposit to the solicitors. She emailed the solicitors asking for their bank details. The reply that came back contained what appeared to be the solicitor's details. She transferred £100,000. A week later the solicitor's completion statement arrived, but her £100,000 transfer was missing. Upon investigation, it was discovered they were incorrect bank details.

Most people do not realise that emails can be intercepted this way.

PREVENTION
- ✓ When setting a new payee for any new payment, transfer £1/$1 and check it arrived by phone and not by email. Most people won't mind and I have never had any complaints from a recipient.

✓ For larger transactions, call up the intended recipient and verify the bank details before making any payments; don't reply an email.

Sending a small amount first also acts as check that you actually entered the correct details and didn't make a typo, especially if you might be in a rush.

1.17 PUSH PAYMENT FRAUD

<u>HOW IT WORKS:</u> The fraudster usually has obtained a lot of information about you prior to calling. The caller will use this to instil confidence that they are genuine. S/He may well have a local accent to further convince you they are genuine. They will be aggressive and have a high sense of urgency.

They want you to transfer money to their account, (because they cannot get online access themselves), to what they call *'a safe account'*. Because you are completing the payment: 'pushing the payment' (hence the name), the bank may not reimburse you.

The overwhelming pressure from the caller convinces you that your bank account is under attack and they are genuine. In some case they pass you onto a supervisor or manager, who is another conspirator and or they will ask you to call back, using the phone number on back of your card.

TIP: Your bank will NEVER ask you to transfer funds to a new *'safe account'*, because they simply don't have enough account numbers available.

TIP: REMEMBER: In the UK when a landline calls a landline and the recipient replaces the handset, <u>the call is not disconnected,</u> fraudsters will play a tune down the phone mimicking a dial tone, so when you pick it up again, you think you are making a fresh call, <u>but miraculously you will be connected back to the same person without going through any switchboard or an automated process.</u>

TIP: Search online and you can hear a recorded live phone conversation of a criminal attempting this fraud. It can also be found on BBC Radio 4 MoneyBox programme archive in episode 6th Sep 2015.
https://www.bbc.co.uk/programmes/b068lsp7

1.18 POSTAL SCAM

HOW IT WORKS: You receive a card in the post (or a text message) from your local postal service for courier, stating there is a £1/$1 short on a package with a phone number to call. Almost everyone can afford to lose a £1/$1. But day or so later, the Fraudsters call pretending to be from your bank stating the delivery card was a scam and starts the Mandate Fraud and says your bank account has been compromised.

1.19 EXAMPLE OF A SCAM POPPING UP IN THE WAKE OF WORLD EVENTS.

CASE STUDY: NEW SCAM IN THE WAKE OF THE COLLAPSE OF THE TRAVEL GIANT THOMAS COOK: *If you receive a phone call offering a refund and asking for your credit card details DO NOT GIVE THEM OUT, IT'S A SCAM.*

The Civil Aviation Authority (CAA) has stated this is not how they operate. The only reason a credit card refund would happen, is if you have asked your card supplier to conduct a charge back under Section 75 of the credit consumer act. And then they don't call, asking for your card number.

TIP: It is standard practice throughout the world for travel agents, to not pay your hotel for your stay until you leave (which I think is wrong, the travel company should pay the hotel on the day of your arrival). As a result, there have been reports of hotels shutting gates and not permitting customers to leave until they pay the hotel their lost money.

Of course, many people at the end of the holiday have run out of money. You should not pay; if in doubt call your own country's embassy.

With that in mind, before every international trip, program the embassy phone number and address into your phone for such contingencies, besides you might have other reasons to call for help e.g., police trouble even when innocent.

TIP: If are pressured into paying a hotel bill, once you have left the hotel, you could report your card lost, assuming you don't need that card on your travel home.

TIP: It is always handy to have a minimum of 2 cards when travelling.

GOLDEN RULES FOR MANY SCAMS:

- ✓ The fraudster will try to create a sense of urgency giving you no time to think.
- ✓ Sob story and/or traumatic event.
- ✓ Creating the scenario that you will lose money if you don't act now.
- ✓ Appeal to your need for money.

REMEMBER THE ABC RULE

A. ASSUME NO ONE IS GENUINE
B. BELIEVE NOTHING YOU HEAR
C. CHALLENGE EVERYTHING
D. DON'T RETURN ANY PHONE CALLS USING NUMBERS SUPPLIED BY THE FRAUDSTER
E. TAKE 5 (5mins) - THINK

FINALLY – ANY SITUATION IN LIFE WHERE YOU ARE PUT UNDER PRESSURE COULD BE A HOAX/SCAM.

2. FRAUDULENT EMAILS & TEXTS – IT IS HOW MOST FRAUDSTERS GAIN ACCESS

Hacking is not easy; it is much easier to let the fraudster in through the back door with a key. This is done by the criminals sending emails and texts that look genuine and you inadvertently click on a link or open an attachment within the email that either:

a) Leads you to a fraudulent website that looks identical to the original in order for them to record your login credentials when you to enter them. (Next step see Cloned Website)

b) Gain access to your device by installing malicious software in the background, which will be either some 'key-logging' software, screen share software or some sort of remote access – a Trojan Horse.

Cyber-crime is likely to only grow as technology advances. The criminals who commit cyber-crime are clever; they go to great lengths and spend time on designing clone websites and phishing emails to look genuine in order for you to fall for their tricks. It is now time to arm yourself with knowledge so you do not become a victim.

DEFINITIONS:

➢ **MALWARE** – is the generic definition of any MALicious softWARE that is used to target you and infect your devices, including: Virus/Worms/Trojans/Spyware/Ransomware/Adware.

➢ **KEYLOGGING SOFTWARE** - software records your keystrokes on the keyboard, which is why many bank logins have procedures where you use a mouse on a drop-down box during the login process.

➢ **SCREEN SHARING SOFTWARE** - allows people to see your screen and watch what you do. I.T. professional use such software to fix your computer remotely; you may have experience of this yourself.

o Both keylogging & screen sharing software are forms of SPYWARE.

➢ **SPAM** - is junk mail: genuine services offered instead of posting flyers through everyone door, which costs money to print and distribute, they are sent via email; they can reach millions of potential customers for free.

- ➤ **SMISHING** - are text messages that appear genuine, hoping you will click on a link or icon within the email, resulting in the fraudster loading malicious software onto your device to record your screen activity or taking you to a fake website that looks so real that you believe it is the genuine website e.g., your bank.
- ➤ **PHISHING (fishing)** – are generally fraud emails that appear genuine, hoping you will click on a link or icon within the email, resulting in the fraudster obtaining a back door into your device or taking you to a fraudster's website that looks so real, that you believe it is the genuine website e.g., your bank.
  - o Pronounced fishing - because they send millions of messages hoping to catch a 'bite'.
- ➤ **SPOOFING** – the fraudsters make any text message or phone call originate from where ever they choose.
  - o E.g., your bank, a local landline number or mobile number so you are tempted to respond.

TEXT MESSAGE WARNING - DURING COVID fraud cases have increased.
It has become apparent that scammers can make any text message or phone call appear to originate from where ever and whomever they like; in essence, you cannot trust any incoming call or text.

TRAP: If you click on the link from a fraudulent text, the criminals will install malicious software on your phone that will record your screen activity. When you access your emails and banking Apps, they will capture your login credentials. Using their own device, they will log in and steal your money.

Once a criminal has gained access to your device, they can do a lot more:
- o Turn on your microphone or camera to watch and listen.
- o Track you.
- o View and steal photos and messages.
- o Send messages to people in your contact list to infect others.
- o Wipe your phone to be inconvenient or destroy the evidence.

WARNING: If your mobile phone is set back to Factory settings or some content has disappeared (Apps / contacts), CONTACT ALL YOUR BANKS IMMEDIATELY to change all passwords, usernames, 5/6-digit passcodes and any other memorable information used as credentials – Mothers Maiden Name (MMN), favourite place, first job etc.

When banking Apps are installed on a new device, there are protocols to follow to ensure you are the correct person. However, for most banks, the same credentials are used when accessing online banking through any web browser.

PREVENTION: – never click on any link supplied on <u>any</u> text message, or open any attachment regardless of whether it appears to be from your bank or not.

TIP: If you are concerned about message being genuine you should contact your bank via your normal method. The best method, being the phone number of the bank of your card, or use the secure message system available with many banks once you are logged in online.

TIP: An indicator that your phone has been compromised, is excessive battery use; the fraudsters link with an APP running in the background, will be a drain on resources.

TIP: Back up your phone regularly, this also helpful when switching phones. If you are unsure how, search on Google/YouTube or ask your phone provider.

TEXT/SMS WARNING – the safest thing to is no matter who the text is from **NEVER EVER click on any link received by text**. Always contact the provider via the number on your bill, back of your card or login online to your account the normal way through your browser or App.

TIP: many fraudulent texts are followed up with a fraudulent phone call in order to sell the text message and hook you.

Remember the fraudster can pretend to be anyone. Here are some other examples.
  ➢ Mobile phone (Cell phone) provider asks you to update your billing details.
  ➢ Your local postal service says there is a £1/$1 shortfall on a parcel you are expecting – works especially around Christmas or national holiday periods.

o This particular scam has been followed up with a fraud phone call pretending to be your bank, informing you that the parcel delivery was a scam and now your bank account has been compromised and the Bank needs to move your money to a safe account. This also is a scam – please see chapter 4 on bank spoof calls.

EMAIL WARNING – if you receive an unsolicited email asking you to reset your password *'due to a security issue'* **DO NOT CLICK ON THE LINK**; login your normal way to change the password. If you believe nothing has been compromised, then ignore it and don't change the password. Think for a moment and ask yourself, "Do I need to change the password?"

TIP: The only time you should click on a password reset link is if you requested it.

MOBILE DEVICES (Tablets & Phones)
One of the biggest problems with mobile devices is you do not have the use of a mouse which is ultimately important to keep yourself protected. If you only use mobile devices without a mouse to access your email, then I suggest using a different app to access them. Some browser apps have a virtual mouse function that you can navigate around your screen which has a left and right click as experienced on a standard desktop/laptop (e.g., Puffin browser available in the app store used to have a mouse). You can always right click and select *Properties* to view.

If you have suspicions about an email, move your mouse to hover over the sender's name or any link within the email and the computer will reveal the true sender's email or web link. Then you can determine its validity. DON'T CLICK IT OR OPEN ANY LINK!

Before we move onto suspicious emails, you need to understand the basic of *domain names*.

A *'domain name',* is the name that appears after 'www.' and in any web address or after the '@' symbol in an email address.
For example, let's say I purchased the domain name 'example.com'. If available, you could purchase 'example.com', 'example.co.uk', 'example.net',

'example.org', 'example.info', 'example.tv' or the new one '.uk'. The '.uk' domain was available for general release in 2019. The list of domain-suffix is almost endless and constantly increasing.

> The web address (also known as a URL) becomes www.example.com
> Email address becomes hello@example.com and you can literally put anything in front of the @ symbol, thus you can create unlimited email addresses.

Popular ones we see are info@example.com, sales@example.com, admin@example.com, no-reply@example.com, mail@example.com.

FRAUDULENT EMAILS

Now that you are armed with the knowledge of domain names, you can view the sender's email to determine its authenticity. All large institutions such as banks will have their main domain for emails from which they send emails.

Here are some main examples:

> PayPal: '@paypal.com', 'PayPal.co.uk' or your own country's equivalent
> Barclays bank: '@barclays.co.uk' or '@barclays.com'
> HSBC bank: '@hsbc.co.uk' or '@hsbc.com'.
> Lloyds Bank: '@lloyds.co.uk' or '@lloyds.com'.
> NatWest: '@natwest.co.uk' or '@natwest.com'.
> Santander: '@santander.co.uk' or '@santander.com'.
> TSB: '@tsb.co.uk' or '@tsb.com'.
> Obviously, these will vary in other countries.
> Apple: '@apple.com'.
> Domino's pizza: '@dominoes.co.uk'.
> Amazon: '@amazon.co.uk' or your home country's variant.
> eBay: '@ebay.co.uk' or your home country's variant.

To name a few.

EXAMPLES OF SUSPICIOUS EMAILS

A genuine email from PayPal will be '@paypal.com' (or your country's variant e.g., '@paypal.co.uk'), any variation on this will likely to be fraudulent. E.g., '@pay_pal.com', '@PayPal.uk.com' etc. Popular fraudulent emails will inform you that your account is suspended, or that there is some other problem with your account.

Examples of fraudulent emails – WARNING the *'from name'* can be made to look like anything, just like a text message can be made to appear from any bank.

- Email from Apple Support – I hovered over the from name 'apple support' which revealed the following email address - [appleservice.noreply-primaryverifyunblocked-id434534557@watreley.com] – is from watreley.com not apple.com.
- Email from Apple telling me someone tried to access my account from Africa - I hovered over the from name 'apple' which revealed the following email address - [noreply4XYG65NI@tidakainspirasi.org] – clearly not from Apple.
- Email from Barclays Bank - [bostjano@delo.si] – the domain is not '@barclays.com' or '.co.uk'.
- Email from TSB Bank - [tsb@eml.co.uk] – should say '@tsb.co.uk'.

You probably get the gist.

SUB-DOMAINS

Now you have learnt about domains for spotting fraudulent email, it is prudent for us to expand on this a little. Companies have many servers to spread the work load, hence many routine emails can come from a different server. To manage this, they put another word in front of the domain separated by a full-stop e.g., if you see the word 'mail' in front of 'paypal.co.uk' to become '@mail.paypal.co.uk', this is an example of sub-domain which is genuine.

Warning; if the word 'mail' and 'PayPal' are separated by a hyphen e.g., 'mail-PayPal.co.uk' - this is not a sub-domain, this is actually a different domain. A sub-domain is only valid if separated by a period (full stop).

If you are ever in doubt, contact the sender via another means; also see solutions below.

SOME MORE EXAMPLES OF SUSPICIOUS EMAILS

Any email from a tax office offering you a refund is pretty much a scam.

CASE STUDY: This is an example below of an email received offering a tax refund from the UK tax office 'HMRC'. Notice:

➢ The email address is mis-spelt, omitting the letter 'C' from HMRC.

> Almost all emails from any government department will have as the end of their domain '.gov.uk' or similar for other countries.
>> o All '.gov' domains are restricted sale and reserved for government departments only.
>> o E.g., Turkey holiday visas come from '.gov.tr'.

EXAMPLE HOAX EMAIL BELOW OFFERING A TAX REFUND
Fig-2.1

> From: HM Revenue & Customs <customer.tax.service@hmr.co.uk>
> Date: 17 October 2018 at 07:25:48 GMT-7

YOU SHOULD DELETE IT IMMEDIATELY WITHOUT CLICKING ON ANY LINKS OR REPLYING.

SOLUTION FOR ANY SUSPICIOUS EMAIL
o Do not reply.
o Do not click on any link contained within the email.
o Do not open any attachments – a virus can be disguised as a PDF, picture file or any file format.
o Do not use any of the information obtained from the suspicious email such as the phone number.
o Do either of the following to verify your account is fine by contacting the company being impersonated:
1. Log into your online account using your normal method i.e., open a new browser window.
2. Start a web chat.
3. Call them with a number you find by logging in or direct from their website.

Once you are verified it is fraudulent, add it to your blacklist. Your email provider will assist you with a blacklist feature.

A SIGN THAT SOMEONE YOU KNOW HAS HAD THEIR EMAIL HACKED FOR SENDING SPAM – fig 2.2.
You may receive an email that will appear from one of your contacts, or someone you know, but

a) The from name 'john smith' won't have an appropriate looking email i.e., it won't look like a sensible name, it will appear to be completely random.
b) The email after the name won't match the email in your address book.
c) The email will just contain a few words and a weird link.
d) A subject name will not bare any resemblance to the email.

The name in the 'from' section is more than likely to be found in your contacts as they have emailed you before. If the email after the name is not visible, you can hover over the link with your mouse to reveal the true sender. Compare it to a genuine email previously received. If you have any doubts, call/text the real person.

Fig-2.2

> **From:** john smith <cax92821@pop12.odn.ne.jp>
> **Sent:** 01 January 2019 00:01
> **To:** xxx
> **Subject:** You got my message
>
> http://cgi.latinol.com/clientes/uinter158/track_clicks.asp?url=https://u.to/BmbYFQ
>
> John

TIP: If you want to be sure, contact the sender.
- Start a fresh email asking if they sent email with the contact.
- Call or text.

But don't forward the suspicious email. They may click on the link themselves becoming a victim.

3. BROWSER AWARENESS & FRAUDULENT CLONED WEBSITES

Fraudsters go to great lengths to scam and steal your hard-earned money. They invest a lot of time to make their fake websites look genuine; hence these scams can be very hard to spot. The most important scam websites to look out for are banking, email, PayPal, or anywhere you intend to enter banking/card details to make purchases or payments.

Web-browsers are programs you use to access the internet. The most popular ones are Google Chrome, Edge, Internet Explorer (IE), Firefox, Safari, Opera, Netscape and AOL, but there are dozens of different ones. Mobile phones often have their own browser software.

ONLINE BANKING
Continuing on from Chapter 2; when you enter your bank details you will be familiar with the section where you are asked to provide some type of security key, or password - for example; 3rd, 5th and 8th character of your memorable work, place, name etc. On a fraudulent website, there will be a subtle sign, after entering your log in details you will be unsuccessful.

On a genuine bank website when you mis-type your memorable word, you will be asked for the same characters when you re-attempt to log in.

On a fraudulent website, when you have an unsuccessful log in attempt, you will be asked for a different set of characters from your memorable word when you re-attempt to log in. They are hoping you think you just mistyped and they will ask you to enter different characters so they can build the picture of your whole memorable word.

There are some things you should never use your search engine to search for - banking is one of them. You should only do the following:

1. Type the address directly into the address bar at the top of your web browser.
2. Create a Bookmark or Favorites in your web-browser.

The address bar is where you see the web address (also known as a URL) starting 'http:\\'
There is more information on 'bookmarks' or 'favourites' later in the chapter.

TRAP: When you start typing within a search engine, some browsers move the typing text up to the address bar; when we start typing in the address bar instead, it assumes it is a search and the results can be confusing. If you find any browser confusing use a different browser.

TIPS: When you search or click on a link, watch for misspelling and replacements; the human brain is clever - when you read a word that has the letters jumbled with the first and last letters in the correct places, you are able to read the words quickly because our brain reads the word as a whole. When reading quickly, it is very easy to miss mis-spelt items. Common characters that are swapped are:

  o   The letter O replaced by the number 0
  o   Upper case i (I) looks identical to lower case L (l)
  o   The letter e is replaced with the number 3

Look out for misspelt websites — they're designed to trick you into downloading malware.
An online scam that can occur on any device or computer; if you accidentally type ".om" instead of ".com," you could find yourself redirected to a web page that wants to install malware, or a back door for fraudsters into your computer.

Examples;

  o   www.netflix.om (real address www.netflix.com)
  o   www.maxzilla.com or www.mozila.com (real address
       www.mozilla.com)
  o   www.barlays.com (real www.barclays.com)
  o   Keep an eye out for extra dashes (-), any domain with a dash is a
       completely different web address.

PROTECTION IS AVAILABLE.
Rapport software to help to verify you are on the right website.

EXAMPLE: After my bank was hacked, it was suggested I install software called 'Trusteer Rapport' by IBM. IBM is probably one of the earliest computer companies in the world. Rapport attaches itself to your browser and shows itself with a green, or grey box at the right-hand corner of the address bar. When you access a bank website for the first time after installation, you will be asked "Do you want to protect this site"? this is a weak point and the first time you access your bank, ensure you are on the correct web page. Once you have protected a web page, next time you visit that page, the software shows a green square on the address bar, indicating you are on the correct website.

The figure below shows a protected and unprotected website.

Fig-3.1

EDITING RAPPORT, you can also manually add or remove web pages from the settings.

An example of a great security feature of Rapport, is when accessing your computer from another computer (known as screen sharing or remote access), Rapport will not permit your bank web page to operate. An example of screen sharing is when you call for computer support and the support line takes control of your computer after directing you to their support web page and you type in a code.

This means that if a fraudster has gained access to your computer via screen sharing, your Rapport software may detect this and prevent your bank web page from working, thus keeping you protected.

Download Rapport here:
http://www.trusteer.com/en/support/rapport-installation-links

OTHER BROWSER SETTINGS

Web browsers are complicated little things, they have a host of features and do a lot in the back ground to make our life easier, record our history and download cookies but they can also allow tracking, websites to track what you do. As our world becomes more digital many of us prefer our privacy.

What are cookies? – These are small data files stored on your PC every time you visit a website. When revisiting frequently used website, they allow the website load images faster, remember usernames, remember our favourite foods for online shopping and even guide targeted advertising which many of us dislike.

History recording is handy. Say you found that item you need/saw a few days ago, last week, last month, well you can find it in your history. To access your history, most browsers have a button, albeit it may be hidden, but most browsers will show your history by pressing CTRL-H together. If your browser is not CTRL-H, search the web "show history in xxx browser"; you will probably see the answer before you finish typing.

HOW TO ACCESS THE BROWSER SETTINGS

You can find an array options within the settings available usually with icon

.

PRIVACY BROWSING

Most browsers have a privacy setting, so the browser will not record your browsing history. Very handy for the following scenarios:
- o Present shopping for a family member on shared device (tablet, laptop, desktop).
- o Booking that holiday whilst at work.
- o Using a device at a friend's house e.g., at a party, checking your bank or social media account.

You can access the private browsing window on most browsers by typing either "Ctrl-Shift-P" or "Ctrl-Shift-N". Some browsers even have an icon you can click 👓. If these don't work, search online "how to turn on private browsing in xxx" for your chosen browser.

When using tablets & phones, you can download from the App/Play store additional browsers. Firefox has two browsers; the standard one plus a second one called Firefox Focus which is a dedicated PRIVACY BROWSER. Firefox focus doesn't record anything. Firefox focus icon is a pink background with a white fox. Standard Firefox has a yellow fox.

Brave browser is another good emerging private browser available www.brave.com. Brave browser is available for windows devices, mac, IOS devices & Android devices.

IOS and Android devices have a vast array of private browsers available. Just search in the App/Play store.

BOOKMARKS or FAVOURITES

Some browsers call them 'Favourites' whilst other browsers call them 'Bookmarks'. From here on I will just say 'bookmarks', but I mean both. As well as being handy for your regular websites, bookmarks are also a good way of protecting you from fraudulent website via web searches. Every time you start a fresh web search you run the risk of ending up on a cloned website.

All browsers have a bookmark bar sitting just below your address bar. It is usually hidden from view by default, but you can turn it on within the settings 'show bookmarks bar'. If you are unsure, just web search "how to show bookmarks on (name the browser you are using)".

The Idea is when is when you know you are on the correct website e.g., your bank or email login, bookmark the page. To bookmark a page, most browsers have a star or heart shaped icon just to the right or left, of your address bar (where you see http://). Most browsers also allow you to add webpages to your bookmark by pressing CTRL-B or CTRL-D.

MISCELLANEOUS POINTS

HAVE YOU EVER WHILST BROWSING

    a) "Thought, I wish it could do that", or "it will would be helpful if it could do that"?

    b) "I hate it when it does that",or "that is so annoying".

Well there is a chance there is a setting that turns off or on a helpful setting. Some of these settings will make you more secure whilst browsing.

Areas of interest:
- Clear browsing data (cashe, history, cookies & temporary internet files).
    - Some browsers can be set to clear browsing data everytime you exit the program.
- Turn off autofill
    - Passwords.
    - Payment information, (stores the credit card or debit card details).
- Block, or warn if you about to visit a harmful website.

Non-security points you can control
- Start up from where you left off (reopens your previous tabs) or a start with fresh page every time.
- Choose where to download files.
- Warn you if you are closing more than one tab.
- Block pop-ups ads.

ADVERTS
Whilst browsing, we often access information. A company makes many from advertisement around its website. Advertising placed on top of a web page which means that is it unlikely that the owner of the website has control over the content and where links will take you.

My best advice is to never click on any adverts. If there is an item that piqued your interest, it is better to open a fresh tab and do search yourself. Just as my advice with certain emails, don't click on the link contained within the email, open a web page and search using the search bar.

Essentially don't trust links supplied by people you don't know, always do your own search.

Remember: links in emails and adverts are usually how fraudsters gain access to your device and start to monitor your browsing data; watching for banking information or other information to steal your identity.

4. SPOOF CALLS - BANKING FRAUD CALLS

SPOOFING – The software exists because it has genuine applications for a government, or helpdesk employee working from home for at least 2 reasons:

> ➤ No matter where they are working in the world, when there is a call back, they will all show the same number so you know who is calling.
> ➤ The callers own contact details are not made public for disgruntled people who want to take retribution.

Previously we covered how your debit and credit cards can be cloned. When your bankcard is cloned, fraudsters don't always use it immediately. You may be watched on CCTV; hence you must always cover your PIN. Frequent travellers have reported having cards cloned several times a year.

When your card is cloned, the fraudster will attempt to purchase items either online, or through a retailer who is also probably be a conspirator, so the retailer will opt for a signature, which then by passes the PIN requirements. Often, when these fraudsters attempt the first transaction, it is for a small amount e.g., £10/$10 before trying larger purchases. I had a card cloned that I had not used for 12 months, then the fraudsters attempted a $1 charity donation before attempting larger amounts.

If your card is cloned and the fraudulent purchase fits within your normal spending pattern, it may well be accepted and the you will first become aware of it will be when you check your bank/credit card statement or online activity. **I suggest reviewing your bank accounts at least monthly.**

GENUINE BANK FRAUD CALL
If the bank thinks they have detected a fraudulent transaction, the bank will make an automated call or, text to you. **This is why it is important that all of your banks and credit card companies have your correct phone number(s).** When the bank initiates an automated fraud call to you:

> ✓ It is generally an automated one, not a person.
> ✓ They will supply you a list of recent transactions – some of them may be genuine.

- ✓ If you recognise all of the transactions, you reply accordingly then you are told there is no further action; this is the end of the matter. There is no need for a person to call you.
- ✓ This is because banks do not want to waste manpower on calls if all your transactions are genuine. They will use automated calls where possible and so do not mistake this genuine call for a fraudulent call.

HUMAN PHONE CALLS TO OR FROM YOUR BANK
- o The fraudsters can choose any number they like to appear on your screen (known as spoofing).
  - o Like most things, technology was developed for genuine applications, e.g., technical support call back, staff can work from home, but for their protection you see the company's phone number.
- o The caller will know a lot about you so they will first supply you with all the information they know, to instill confidence.

RESPONDING TO CALLS FROM YOUR BANK- REAL OR SUSPICIOUS:
- o DON'T PANIC. Take your time - there is no rush.
- o NEVER give out over the phone a One-Time-Passcode (OTP) received on your phone.
- o NEVER give out your full security details when you call the bank.
- o NEVER give out your PIN.
- o NEVER transfer money to another account because of fraud called 'safe account'.
- o NEVER give out any part of your login details for your *phone banking/online banking/mobile App.*

FOLLOW UP ACTION
- ✓ REMEMBER: In the UK when a landline calls a landline and the recipient replaces the handset – THE CALL IS NOT DISCONNECTED – fraudsters will play a tune down the phone mimicking a dial tone, so when you pick it up again, you think you are making a fresh call.
- ✓ If you are suspicious about a call, inform the caller you will call back – they won't mind.
- ✓ Don't use any of the phone numbers supplied by the potential fraudster.

- o The same principle applies to any suspicious emails or letters in the post.
- ✓ Use a different phone, line to call the bank back if you have access to one.
- ✓ If you don't have access to another phone, either:
  - o Wait an hour before trying to call your bank (this is official bank advice).
  - o Try to call a friend, or family member first to ensure the phone line is free and not still occupied by the fraudster.

OTHER SPOOF CALLS AND TEXTS

You just understood how fraudsters use genuine software to make their phone number appear to be your bank's number. Computers can dial hundreds of phone numbers per second and if they get a 1% answer rate, they are doing well.

Fraudsters also use computers to make automated calls, with a mechanical voice warning of a problem that needs your attention; some examples are:
- o "Your internet has been compromised".
- o "Suspicious activity on your amazon or eBay account" or any other online account.
- o "DVLA or DMV issues".
- o The list is endless of possible scams, it is impossible to keep up with them all.

Fraudsters now have the technology to spoof text messages. They often pre-empt a scam call with a text. When you receive spoof texts, they will appear at the bottom of any genuine conversation thread. This spoof text is called 'SMISHING'

TIPS
- ✓ **Pretty much any call asking you to press number one or any other number is most likely to be a scam.**
- ✓ **Generally only law enforcement has the power to issue a warrant for your arrest, certainly tax offices do not.**
- ✓ **Genuine calls are calm and won't mind you calling back.**
- ✓ **Fraudulent calls are generally aggressive with urgency to get you to act without thinking.**

Many people who are scammed realise it the moment they hang up the phone, because there is no more urgency and they are thinking clearly. Often it is too late. <u>Still contact your bank immediately, they may be able to recover some of your money.</u>

Some banks and tax authorities are trying to use of software to prevent their phone number from being used, but the criminals are clever, so you cannot rely on this to be effective.

I can only reiterate, take a minute, don't be rushed, contact the company via a number you find on your statement, back of your bank card, websites. Don't trust anyone on the end of phone.

No one losses money by saying no.

---

5. BANKING & CARD USE

INFORMATION ABOUT BANK TRANSFERS
Until very recently, you may not be aware that when transferring money or paying a bill, the name on the receiving account did not need to match the account number; some banks currently do not check these against the recipient's name. Test this yourself; transfer £1/$1 to another family member, but enter a fictitious name e.g., Mickey Mouse. The major banks rectified this; it is called *'Account Name Verification'*. It was implemented in 2020. **WARNING**: It may take time before it is mandatory for all banks, but other countries may have different protocols and procedures.

TIP: This account name verification should prevent mandate fraud, or push payment fraud mentioned earlier in the book. Still never transfer money to a 'safe account'.

TRAP: If the criminal has opened an account with a similar name, you might accept the suggestion the bank offers when making payment. It generally won't apply to international payments; not all banks have this operational yet; as new banks emerge; it may take time to be fully effective and it may not be available in your country.

TRAP: Fraudsters will also give some reason to say the account name verification is not currently working and to proceed with the transfer.

DEFINITIONS:
- ➢ Phone banking - refers to when you actually call your bank.
- ➢ Online and mobile banking - refers to when you access your accounts online whether it through a browser, or App. Phone apps are part of the online banking.

DEBIT & CREDIT CARDS
We have been discussing debit/credit card fraud in the form of card cloning and it is impossible to predict or prevent. It only takes a rogue employee to sell your data, or wherever you have shopped, the retailer is hacked.
However, iit is possible to limit the damage.

Bankcards are cloned in one of three ways:
1. The staff member quickly scans the card with a device under their apron or trouser leg, usually with the rouse of dropping your card.
2. A staff member behind the scenes (e.g., admin staff) sells your details to a criminal.
3. The merchant (the operator of the card machine) could be hacked.

Items 1 and 2 are the more likely. The BBC programme 'The Real Hustle' demonstrates this in many episodes. **The program can be found on BBC3 and many episodes are available on YouTube.**

TIP: Using PayPal with online retailers & service providers, can be effective because the retailer does not see your card number, hence it cannot be cloned.

TIP: See the chapter on Passwords and Domain Names for further advice regarding PayPal.

TIP: If you lose sight of your bankcard - when it is handed back to you **DOUBLE CHECK IT IS YOUR CARD.** Check your name on the front. Aside from this, there is a high-risk area of card cloning, they may have just stolen your card and returned to you a look-a-like.

➤ If a staff member drops your card, observe carefully. It takes a fraction of a second for them to skim / clone it.
➤ If the staff member says the PIN card terminal is not working and offers to get another one - **ASK FOR YOUR CARD BACK FIRST** and do not take 'NO' for an answer, or accompany the staff member to the till to pay for your meal – the key here is, do not let your card leave your sight.
➤ In all honesty, there is no reason why staff should handle your card at all. It is possible for you to insert & remove it yourself. Proactive retailers' train their staff to say "please insert the card yourself". Some countries are very strict about staff not handling your card – other countries might not be so, so be aware of this.

PIN (PERSONAL IDENTIFICATION NUMBER)

Card details are more valuable with your PIN; rogue employees and criminals do review CCTV in order to obtain it. Many people do not cover their PIN when at the till, or at the ATM. Speaking for myself, I have been waiting in a queue and seen a PIN being entered. This carelessness will put you at risk. Ensure that you cover your hand when entering your PIN at all times.

Some countries have a culture where you raise the PIN pad to your face whilst entering your PIN. In the UK, most PIN terminals sit in a cradle. What many people do not realise is most PIN terminals can be easily lifted out to use. If a PIN terminal cannot be removed, it's advisable to cover your hand with your wallet to enter your PIN by touch. The number 5 is always raised for people with vision impairment so you can feel where you are.

TIP: If you cannot see your own PIN, there is a good chance no one else can either.

I adopt the same strategy for ATM use. Criminals install small button size cameras to record your PIN entry as well as installing an almost invisible sleeve over the card slot to record your card details. At least if you cover your hand whilst entering you PIN, and if your card is copied, its use is limited without the PIN.

ATM TIPS:

- ➢ A small device might be fitted just over the card aperture that reads the card on the way in.
- ➢ It might be a sleeve that is fitted into the card slot.
- ➢ It might be a bigger cover the covers the card display.
- ➢ Any camera is likely to be a covert camera such as a button-cam.
- ➢ The area may be covered by CCTV.

- ✓ Do give a second glance.
- ✓ Even run your finger around the card slot.
- ✓ Are there any loose-fitting parts?
- ✓ Give anything a wiggle.
- ✓ Do be wary if the card is ejected prematurely especially if you have not entered your PIN.
- ✓ Do be wary if your card is kept when you know there is nothing wrong with your account – contact the bank immediately.

TIPS

✓ After inserting your card, if the ATM doesn't react as it should normally or has an undue delay; it may be a sign the ATM has been tampered with.

✓ ATM's say "out of order" when they are out of cash, so if your card is returned without dispensing any cash, the ATM may have been tampered with.

✓ Remember; If you cannot see your own PIN, there is a good chance no one else can either.

ATMs located in secluded areas with less traffic, or the lack of any obvious CCTV; have a higher risk of being tampered with. High street or main bank ATMs within CCTV areas may be safer to use, but remember not to be complacent - cover your PIN entry. **There were reports on social media of local residents having their card cloned from an ATM located on the property of a well-known international convenience store chain.**

The saying that, *if you are being forced to withdraw money at the ATM and if you enter your PIN in reverse, it will alert the police*, unfortunately this is a myth. **Your life is more important; I suggest you comply with any demands and report it to the police as soon as you are safe**. The police may be able to track the thief on CCTV and you may be able to claim against your house insurance policy. Many house insurance policies cover the theft of a limited amount of cash on your person when outside the home. In order to make any successful claim, you will need to report it to the police and obtain a crime number.

SIGNING YOUR CARDS

With chip and PIN being so widely used globally, many people are of the opinion that signing your bankcard is no longer necessary. This is not the case.

1. Banking instructions enclosed with your card still instruct you to sign your card upon its arrival. If you don't and you are a victim of fraud, **the bank may refuse to reimburse you**, citing that you were careless.
2. Visa and MasterCard guidelines state 'an unsigned card is invalid'.
3. If your card is stolen or lost, the individual could sign it themselves and impersonate you in the bank.

4. Some retailers still require a signature for refunds in conjunction with, or instead of your PIN. You are not permitted to sign the card in front of the retailer because you may have just stolen it.
5. PIN terminals using satellite linkups, or broadband do not work 100% of the time. If you happen to be in a shop at the precise moment, it does not authorise, you may be asked to sign. If your card is unsigned, you will not be permitted to sign your card in front of the retailer.
    a. Odds are it will occur when you are in a rush.
    b. Also, many chip and PIN cards do not work when travelling outside the country of issue and revert to signatures.
    c. Poorer countries technology is also not as reliable.
6. Some retailers still require a signature for refunds in conjunction with, or instead of your PIN. You are not permitted to sign the card in front of the retailer because you may have just stolen it.

CASE STUDY TRUE STORY: In June 2018 the VISA network went down throughout much of Europe for several hours one Friday afternoon leaving millions of consumers without any means of payment at the till. Any retailer who held onto the manual card machines from the 80's or 90's, were taking payments with a signature.

CASE STUDY TRUE STORY: Recently, I was asked for a signature in order to receive a refund; I had genuinely forgotten to sign my card. As a result, the retailer refused my refund and I had to return again later as he wouldn't permit me to sign it in front of him.

Some people don't sign their card for fear that it could expose them to fraud. In reality card fraud happens but it is not because of the signature on the card. It is safe to sign your card which is why there is still a space to do so.

CREDIT/DEBIT CARDS and PayPal
You may be aware that by paying with your credit card in the UK, you benefit from Section 75 of the Credit Consumer Act 1974 whereby if you don't receive a refund from the retailer, or service provider, the credit card company has to reimburse you by law. Note that this only applies to purchases between £100 & £30,000; items under £100 are not coverable.
Some banks offer a similar service with payments made by debit cards (known as the debit card charge-back). This is not backed by the law, so is voluntary.

The use of PayPal can give you protection, no matter which payment method you use. If you have a dispute, try to establish contact with the retailer/service provider first; log your calls, emails and social media posts. If no redress, commence a dispute with PayPal, they will give the retailer a nudge, to respond; if there is no or inadequate response, PayPal will refund you and charge back the retailer. This can be very effective for those smaller purchases.

Most bills we pay are on Direct Debit or Standing Order, but there is a 3rd billing option *continuous card authority*. For those that do not know the difference:

- **Direct debit**: the company pulls the money from your bank and they can vary the amount and date; typical for mortgages, utilities, insurances etc.
- **Standing order**: you the bill payer controls the payment to the payee, the payee cannot vary the amount, date or cancel the payments. This is typical for rent payments or regular transfers between your own accounts.
- **Continuous card authority**: this is where you pay a regular bill but the provider bills your debit/credit card every month. Netflix take their payments this way. These are harder to stop, you have to contact the bill company e.g., Netflix to ask them to stop taking money.

DEBIT CARD vs. CREDIT CARD WHEN YOU SUFFER A FRAUD

If you pay with a credit card and suffer a fraud:
- ➢ You have protection in law from the Credit Consumer Act;
- ➢ When you suffer fraud, you don't have to pay for it, it sits there as a balance whilst you dispute it.
- ➢ You are not deprived of your money during the investigation.
- ➢ The credit card company will usually not charge interest on that balance whilst being disputed.

If you pay with a debit card and suffer a fraud:
- ➢ You could be deprived of your money during the dispute resolution/investigation until it is refunded.
- ➢ This could be tough if don't have much money; the knock-on effect could be catastrophic if you have bills that need paying.

ORGANISING YOUR BANKING – COMPARTMENTALISATION TO LIMIT DAMAGE IF A CARD IS CLONED

Having your banking compartmentalised and organised can limit your exposure should you be a victim of fraud with card cloning. By organising your banking into different accounts, you ensure your most important money for savings, mortgage/rent payments etc. are not exposed.

➢ Bills account (with a debit card).
➢ Savings account (no overdraft or debit card).
➢ Spending or spends account (with a debit card but no overdraft).
➢ Current account for all *continuous card authorities*. (with a debit card but no overdraft).
➢ Property account for rental income and expenditures (helps prepare tax returns).
➢ Business account for business income and expenses (helps prepare tax returns).
  ○ This doesn't have to be an actual business bank account, just using a separate personal account does the same job.
  ○ Having said that, you have access to additional services with a business bank account, as well as overdraft interest in the UK is cheaper than an overdraft with a personal account.

Apart from helping to budget and manage your finances, it will help restrict any losses should you fall victim with my safety tips below, because you don't need to carry all your cards with you all the time.

SAFETY TIPS:
➢ If the savings account doesn't have a debit card, it can't be cloned or stolen.
➢ The bills account debit card:
  ○ Never leaves the house – the card cannot be lost, stolen or skimmed by an employee.
  ○ Never used online or on the phone – the card cannot be cloned or sold to fraudsters.
  ○ This way you are not putting your money to pay the mortgage/rent and bills at risk.

- ➢ If your <u>spending account or continuous card authority account</u> debit card is lost/stolen/cloned, you have backup cards whilst you wait for your replacements.
- ➢ If the <u>spending account</u> & <u>continuous card authority account</u> do not have an overdraft facility, there is a limit to how much they can get.
- ➢ <u>Spending account</u>: I transfer a small amount into my spending account monthly £250/$250 via a standing order; once it's gone, it's gone, I wait until next month before more money goes in as it helps with budgeting and control your spending.
- ➢ <u>Continuous card authority account:</u> I have a separate account solely for my *continuous card authorities*. My Netflix money goes in 3-days before Netflix takes their money using a *continuous card authority.*
  - o Allow 3-days in case of weekends. If your billing date is the 15th and this month the 15th is a Sunday, they may attempt to bill you on Sunday before your money goes in Monday, in which case your funds need to be there Friday or it won't go through and you will have your services suspended; this happened to me.
  - o Otherwise, this separate bank account sits there with a balance of £10/$10 as a buffer.
- ➢ I use a separate account for *continuous card authorities* so it runs automatically with standing order payments in and the retailer payments out. Thus, because I put £250/£250 into my spending account each month and if a supplier on my gets trigger happy early in the month and attempts to take more money, there is none.
  - o TRUE STORY: *2021, I was ordering online from a new company that I had not previously used, so I transferred funds into the bank account I use for 'continuous card authorities' and paid online, over the next few days, they attempted another five payments, but as the account sits with just £10, the card was declined. I know because every time the card was declined, I received a text alert from my bank.*
- ➢ By having a *spends account* which I carry the debit card daily and my *continuous card authority* account that stays at home, if either card is compromised, I can use the other card by moving money, without risking the money in my other accounts, especially savings and bills account.

- If you have little in the way of savings, being hit by card fraud may severely disrupt your life. So, whilst you may not need or want extra accounts, at least have two accounts to keep yourself protected.
  - Bills accounts & Spending account preferably with different banks (see TIP below).
- The cards I don't need day-to-day, are locked in a safe.

TIP: Occasionally, banks have problems, IT issues, hacked, financial problems, recession, pandemics and during these various crises, sometimes you can't access your own money for several hours, days or even weeks. If you have at least one account with another bank you can have access to some money.

TIP: Earlier in the chapter, I mentioned how retailers relied on signatures when the VISA network went down for many hours. For this reason, if you have one or more bank accounts with a different bank, choose a bank that uses the MASTERCARD network instead of VISA, so you are hedging your bets. The same applies to credit cards or prepaid cards, if you use either or both, have one with VISA and one with MASTERCARD.

CARD PAYMENT ONLINE & OFFLINE TIPS
- ✓ Pay for all online activity with a credit card where possible.
- ✓ Consider using a prepaid card, if you do not have a credit card. (some prepay cards have fees).
- ✓ If you don't have either of these, consider a spare bank account, or open a new bank account just for online purchases but ensure it has no overdraft facility. Yes, it is a little hassle when making payments to ensure it has money, better that than losing the money you cannot afford to lose.
  - If opening a new account, open two so you can create your spends and continuous card authority accounts.
- ✓ Generally, I never use any debit card for online transactions; if I am paying for a government service that does not allow credit cards e.g., passport application, I will transfer the funds into my separate account used for my 'continuous card authorities' and pay with this debit card.
- ✓ Don't use your debit card linked to your savings or bills account.

PAYPAL

PayPal is a digital wallet; you register your debit or credit cards; when you are at an online checkout you may see the PayPal symbol, you are directed to the PayPal page (or a PayPal window may pop up), login and select which card you wish to pay with, then you are redirected back to the vendor's site.

The big advantage of PayPal is that the vendor does not see your actual card number, so it cannot be cloned or sold.

PayPal allows you to register multiple debit/credit cards as well as bank accounts, which you can choose different payment methods for each transaction; e.g., personal or business / debit or credit card.

Login into PayPal and go to your Wallet – here you can add, remove and edit cards, or connected bank accounts within your PayPal account.

Now imagine your PayPal account is hacked. The fraudster has potentially had access to all of the funds linked to your wallet. Under normal protocol, you cannot see your full card number of the cards in your wallet, so should your PayPal account become compromised, your card(s) should not, but these cyber-criminals are very clever people and they may be able to reveal the full card details.

PayPal TIPS

1. Register a credit card instead of debit cards or bank accounts where possible.
2. Don't register any debit card or bank accounts that contain important money (savings or bills a/c).
3. Only register one card, you can always transfer money to account registered with PayPal before using PayPal.
4. Don't use the same password as eBay, our eBay was hacked then they hacked our PayPal.
5. If your PayPal is hacked, you may need to cancel the cards you have registered in your wallet.

NOTE: If you close your PayPal account, you will lose all entire purchase history, but the purchase history is handy for items under warranty such as electrical items.

There are further protection protocols regarding PayPal by having more than one account, within the domain section later in the book.

PHONE/TABLET BANKING Apps
They are very safe, like an encrypted worm hole directly to your bank. This because you have to verify yourself when setting it up with a combination of: SMS codes to your phone, PIN card reader, or a code at an ATM.

They are generally safer than using a browser on your device, or computer. Access through a browser is usually required for more non-regular tasks, such as: Secure messages, order placement cards when damaged, setting up a new payee, downloading statements etc. are just some of the items unavailable on some Apps.

When in public the mobile data is very secure and should be favoured over public Wi-Fi. More detailed guidance is available in later chapters.

Some anti-virus/internet security programs have additional features to help protect you. This is very handy if you are banking on your own laptop in a public area and using public Wi-Fi. My anti-virus/internet security provides a separate mini-program. When it is runs, it opens a secured encrypted browser.

Fig-5.1

Keep it handy by dragging it into the taskbar at the bottom of your screen. When activated, it opens a new SECURED browser page window (even when browser is already open) and may show a confirmation message; see below.

Fig-5.2

This is used every time I access my bank, credit card or PayPal account online.

VIRTUAL CARDS

Another great emerging idea is a virtual card. A virtual card is where the banking App provides a set of card details either online or through the banking App: card number, expiry date & CVV code from the back of the card. They are completely separate to physical your debit or credit card.

The idea of virtual cards is not new, online banks introduced them in the early 00's. They are now re-emerging with online banks and also with prepaid cards. I have a prepaid card that I like to use in new companies; it comes with a physical chip & pin card including contactless payments as well as a virtual card that I can view within the App.

The idea is you use the VIRTUAL CARD for all ONLINE purchases, should a rogue member of staff steal your card details, the virtual card number can be cancelled with a new one being issued quickly, without compromising your physical card so you still have access to your funds.

6. PHONE APPLICATIONS OR APPS

In today's world, we all use apps on our phone, from shopping sites, to social media and emails to banking. We are all guilty at times of staying logged into some social media, shopping site, email etc. because it is so quick and efficient to pop in and out of it. Fortunately, sensitive sites like banking tends to log you out automatically after a period of non-activity; some do not.

Whether on your PC or tablet at home or out, when not in use you should physically log out: closing the app is not the same as logging out.

Advantages
  i.   If your phone is lost/stolen, cloned, hacked through Wi-Fi or blue-jacked (blue-jacking is where someone hacks your phone through the Bluetooth connection), there is a lot the criminals can do when you remain logged into social media or email. Further elaboration below.
  ii. It forces you to use your passwords more often and help commit them to long-term memory; when you are not typing your password regularly enough, one tends to forget them.
  iii. It saves your battery and data allowance.

Item i. above; assumes one of the events above occur and you are logged into various apps, the criminals can:
  a) Check a delivery address to see where you live.
  b) If travelling, they know you are not at home and can sell on your details; airport baggage handlers have been known to sell your address to criminals when displayed on a luggage label.
  c) View payment details and obtain your card details, then go on to clone your card.
  d) View saved networks; now they have your home and/or work Wi-Fi password to hack it.
  e) Gain access to your emails. Once accessed, they can reset all other passwords.
  f) Possible banking details.

Item ii. above; a prime example would be when you use your social media of choice at home on your tablet/phone, so you remain logged in without ever logging out. When we travel overseas and connect to the hotel Wi-Fi, you find you are auto-logged out; whether it detected it was a foreign network, air travel or powering off is unknown, but the snag is you can't remember your password.

The problem is if your phone is lost or stolen, you may have the sense to change all your associated passwords along with forcing all devices to log off and re-login, not forgetting the home Wi-Fi but what about if your device is cloned or hacked? You won't know they have access until it is too late.

Do not rely on your phone passcode to keep you protected. With the right software a criminal will connect via a cable and your phone can be hacked.

If you truly feel that logging out is really too cumbersome, then at least be smart enough to pick the right moments when you should log out; when the risk of theft and cloning is higher like:
- When attending a party.
- Festivals.
- Train/bus terminals.
- Airports.
- Large public areas e.g., Trafalgar square.
- Whilst on holiday.

LOG OUT AND STAY SAFE

7. STAYING SAFE ON Wi-Fi

Later in the book within the chapter on 'Routers', you will see how to change your Wi-Fi name, hence criminals will create their own Wi-Fi in public areas with the same, or similar name as another genuine Wi-Fi or even make one up.

CASE STUDY: *You are at the airport which does not offer an airport-wide free Wi-Fi, as all the retailers have their own Wi-Fi for customers, so the fraudster creates one, e.g., "Airport Wi-Fi".*

Once on the criminal's Wi-Fi, they will be able to:
➤ View all the web pages you are viewing.
➤ Watch and record you enter any passwords.
➤ Remotely activate your microphone and camera.
➤ Install software on your device (phone/tablet/laptop) without you knowing, which can send information back to the criminal which passwords you use.

GOLDEN RULES:
✓ Never do sensitive things whilst on public Wi-Fi; banking, credit cards, emails etc. If you do need to do login to confidential areas, consider disconnecting from the Wi-Fi and using your mobile data.
✓ Mobile data is extremely secure and your data traffic is encrypted. Not impossible but either your phone or phone network would have to be hacked first.
✓ If it is urgent and you have to use the Wi-Fi, <u>never tick the box to show your password and ensure you always log out</u>.
✓ If you are using a hotel Wi-Fi for social media or emails, always log out again when not using them. If your phone is hacked during your stay, the fraudster will wait until your phone is not in use to take control. More on this subject in chapter 6.

PUBLIC Wi-Fi vs. MOBILE DATA
The majority of the time, when accessing online banking on your phone within the same country as your SIM card was issued, the phone will use your 3G/4G connection; and the connection is encrypted. At times we use Wi-Fi on our phones. Any public Wi-Fi is not secure, meaning someone else on the Wi-Fi

could hack your device, watch what you do and obtain any password you may use. Just because you enter a Wi-Fi password to access the Wi-Fi does not mean it is a secured network.

Banking, emails, remote computer access or any other highly sensitive areas should never be done on a public Wi-Fi; for these tasks, turnoff Wi-Fi to use your mobile data for such tasks.

Virtual Private Network (VPN)
If you need to access sensitive areas whilst using public Wi-Fi, consider using a Virtual Private Network (VPN). A VPN is a program that encrypts your data transmission whilst online. If you are hacked whilst using Wi-Fi, the criminals cannot see what you are doing or read any of your data. VPN's have other features too, but are not relevant here.

There are VPN apps for mobile devices and software you can install on a desktop pc. It is also handy if you live in a shared living space, or share your router with lodgers. Although for lodgers, I suggest creating a guest network; see Guest Network under **Routers**.

VPN Pointers
- ✓ They are not expensive and any reasonable cost is worth it against what you could lose if your device is compromised.
- ✓ Many VPN licences cover multiple devices; worth considering if you wish to protect several devices.
- ✓ Some VPN programs have a version that can be installed on Laptops and Desktops for Macs and Windows.
- ✓ Read any reviews, specifications & features to ensure the program you choose covers all of your requirements above.
- ✓ They are also very easy to use.

Search within the App store or Play store for a VPN.

When turning on the VPN, you have the option to choose at alternate location (one of its features), meaning you can actually choose to appear to be in another country. It does this by giving you different IP address; this may cause a minor conflict.

TRAP: Some on demand streaming services for TV/Film, know when you are using a VPN and will not permit streaming services; it is all to do with licence permissions in different countries.

TIP: Turn on the VPN to login (you will be able to browse the full menu just not actually watch anything) then turn off the VPN to commence watching if it prevents you from watching. Remember whilst the VPN is off, do not do anything else. Once you have finished watching your program, turn you VPN back on.

Some browsers have a built in VPN but it may not be as robust; I recommend purchasing your own. They are very easy to use – free help will be available from the provider through their support/customer service.

TIP: As mobile data gets cheaper; you can increase your mobile data plans. Most smart phones can create your own mobile hotspot (your own personal Wi-Fi to connect your devices to). **REMEMBER**: mobile data is encrypted, so unless your phone has been compromised from a fraudulent text, it will be virtually impenetrable.

8. PASSWORDS

Arguably the most difficult task is how to decide what criteria you will use to create your passwords. In this increasingly digitalised society, there is an increasing need to rely on more logins than the average person can be expected to remember.

1. Have a pen and paper handy to write some notes along the way.
2. Google top 500 passwords. You will be amazed at what is on this list. These include 'qwerty', 'zxcvb', 'asdfg', the word 'password' etc.
3. If you use any on this list, write them on the paper above. These are the ones you need to change ASAP; also note where you use them.

Cyber-criminals have programs that can run the top 500 passwords in a matter of seconds, so you must avoid them at all costs.

WHY ARE PASSWORDS SO IMPORTANT?
We have so many passwords to remember, we naturally use the same password for multiple logins. Therefore, some hackers target retailers and other institutions as their security tends to be not as good as financial institutions etc.

Once a hacker has breaches, a company that holds passwords, the hackers will naturally use those credentials in as many other online companies as they can think of, Emails, banks & credit cards, eBay, PayPal, Amazon etc. as well as sell those details on the 'dark web'.

Here are some of the top data breaches in the 21st century and their impact:
- Yahoo – 3 billion users
- Adult friend finder – 412 million users
- My Space – 360 million users
- Equifax – 147 million consumers
- LinkedIn – 165 million users
- eBay – 145 million customers
- Curry's Pcworld (UK) was hacked 2018 impact unknown.

Most countries have a strict Data Protection Laws, which requires strict rules about notifying the regulatory body of data breaches. In the UK this is 72 hours after a breach has been discovered.

When any institution realises that they have a data breach, you the customer will be notified fairly quickly; once you have been notified of a data breach you should:

➤ Not use any link in the email; same principle applies.
➤ Change your password; login using your normal means e.g., bookmark or type the URL into the address bar.
➤ Consider all the other online places you have used the same username and password as the company that has just been breached.

PASSWORD STRUCTURE

As there are so many passwords to remember, perhaps you may find it useful to implement a hierarchal structure or tiered level as shown below. When creating a new structure for passwords, it may be helpful to write it all down in a tree format. Ensure you shred any of your notes afterward.

TIER 1

Low-level, Simpler password using characters and numbers (alpha-numeric): Perhaps used in areas that don't involve money and places where card details are not stored; e.g., loyalty card points or online shopping sites which do not store card details. Many people use one password for everything including banking, but here, use one password for these non-financial items.

TIER 2

Mid-level, complexity: Think about replacing some letters for numbers, e.g., "1" for the letter "l" or "3" for the letter "e" etc. Also, mix upper and lower case, don't just simply make the first letter upper case, consider other letters (first and last) or for each new syllable.

TIER 3

Top-level password using symbols as well as alpha-numeric, for platforms like eBay, Amazon, PayPal, which store card information and obviously banking. Your emails must also be a Tier 3 type password.

Some websites including some banking or email providers don't always permit symbols, so you may need to beef up your Tier 2 password.

TIER 4 individual (Tier 3)
There are some places that should have their own individual password not used anywhere else for your protection:

1. Emails; if the fraudster hacks your email, they can reset anything they like whilst freezing you out, making it so much harder for you to regain control.
2. Banking; if you bank with more than one bank, use a different set of security info for the different banks; if the fraudster gains access to one bank account and identify transfers to/from your other bank accounts you use, they will try their luck on your other accounts; will they get lucky!
3. Any other very sensitive areas e.g., PayPal, work login, remote pc access etc.

Work-related items should be a completely separate set of passwords; if either home or work is compromised, the other is not.

PASSWORD MANAGER
Nowadays with so many passwords to remember, we have to use some multiple times usually with the same email address, so if one place is hacked and they obtain your details, they will try the same email and password on many other sites to see where they can get into.

A password manager is a program usually installed on your computer/laptop/tablet/phone, or it is an 'add-on' to your web browsers.

You control the password manager with a master password so only one to remember.

TYPICAL FEATURES: (not all password managers will have the same features)
➤ Remember all your passwords that you choose.
➤ Auto-prompt to save any new password – you can turn the auto-prompt off and on.

- ➢ Turn off the auto-prompt for specific sites e.g., banking, if you prefer to remember these yourself.
- ➢ Work across multiple operating systems and web browsers – certainly covers the main ones: IE, Firefox, Chrome, Opera, Safari, as well as some lesser-known ones, e.g., Avent (very light browser also works from a USB drive).
- ➢ Create complex passwords, by selecting options:
  - o Length
  - o Caps vs. no caps
  - o Numbers
  - o Symbols
- ➢ It can save all the boxes on a website for use with regular form filling; e.g.
  - o You purchase online a lot and are fed up with entering your name, address, post code etc.
  - o A solicitor completing land registry forms that has fields that are the same for every client.
  - o An accountant completing tax returns that has fields that are the same for every client.
- ➢ Control how long you remain logged-in, plus allow an auto-logout when the screen saver activates or your device screen timeout.
- ➢ Can sync across multiple devices if you wish to.

ADVANTAGES
- ✓ Creating a completely unique password for everything, resulting in no passwords are duplicated.
- ✓ Helps you remember every online account you have. You can review ones not used in a long time and request your account to be closed, which is much easier with new data protection laws.
- ✓ Excluding banking and email logins, only one password to remember.

CHOOSING YOUR PASSWORD MANAGER
I would use various websites to review feedback and professional advice, also reviewing their features as some may vary. You would use websites such as:
- ➢ Which
- ➢ TechRadar
- ➢ PCmag
- ➢ Wired

➤ Plus, many more. Do your research.

Factors in choosing:
> ➤ Where are your passwords stored; on your local device, in the cloud or both?
> ➤ Stored on your device will mean syncing across other devices a little more difficult but arguable safer.
> ➤ Price of purchase.

Password managers I have heard of are, but I have no experience with them all.
> ➤ Dashlane
> ➤ Keeper
> ➤ Last Pass
> ➤ RoboForm
> ➤ KeePass (spelt correctly)
> ➤ But there are many more. Do your research.

TRAP: As with my advice on the Mobile Apps chapter, don't remain logged into your password manager, or you will leave yourself exposed.

TIP: Keep auto-log off period short and ensure the auto-log off with screen timeout or when the screen saver is enabled.

PASSWORD GENERAL TIPS TO CONSIDER
1. The use of the £ symbol within your passwords, many keyboards from other countries do not have a £ sign; invariable where cyber-crime may be perpetrated.
2. Use data from your childhood, it is already within your long-term memory and it is difficult to verify (harder for the fraudsters to guess, unless on social media).
3. Past postcodes: UK ones are alpha-numeric and throw in a symbol; perhaps a previous address with some significance, e.g., a first house with your baby, first property purchase. If you do forget it, it is possible to look it up.
4. Previous suburbs you lived in; A suburb is a local area within a city. Suburbs for many places are not part of the formal postal address. Example of a suburb:

    a.   Greenwich is a Suburb of London.

    b.   Manhattan is a Suburb of New York City.

5.   You can also use a random word generator available online for free.

6.   Some logins require a 5-digit code. If you live in the United States, or have family there, you will know 5-digit postcodes are used. I have known people to use;

    a.   Part of their Social Security number.

    b.   Part of their employee I.D.

    c.   Part of their Forces ID number.

    d.   Part of their first or last set of numbers from their debit/credit card to which the bank relates.

    e.   The code on the back of their driving licence.

    f.   Part of their passport number.

7.   All these numbers are hard for fraudsters to discover, but if you forget the actual characters or digits, you can look them up; when your passport/licence is renewed, change the login.

JUST DON'T TELL ANYONE YOUR SYSTEM – IF YOU EVER HAVE A BREACH, CHANGE YOUR SYSTEM

CASE STUDY: *I heard one elderly person say, "because the last 4-digits are visible when I insert my card, I always use those". This is a fine technique but you don't say it aloud in a busy shop.*

9. ROUTER & HOME NETWORK

FREE HELP IS AVAILABLE FROM YOUR INTERNET SERVICE PROVIDER (ISP).

Your router at home or work, whether supplied by your Internet provider, or one you purchased yourself, has a vast array of features you probably never knew existed. If you use a router not provided by your Internet Provider, the technical assistance may be limited. These days, the routers supplied by your internet provider are generally very good.

NOTE: There are vast arrays of commercial routers as well as ones supplied by your ISP. We cannot cover all makes and models here, so the idea is to introduce ideas in order for you to explore with your instruction manuals. Don't forget your ISP can supply additional support, usually free of charge.

TIP: Often when we apply changes to any router, it undertakes a reset (like a mini-reboot), so all connections are temporarily interrupted; anyone online in the house may lose internet connection, problematic if they are working online with unsaved data or streaming a TV services such as Netflix; so, pick your moments when you choose to change your router settings.

Chapter Sections
1. How to access your routers admin settings
2. How to change your admin and Wi-Fi passwords
3. Router security
4. SSID (Service Set Identifier; aka your routers Wi-Fi's name that is broadcasted for other computers to see when you search for Wi-Fi)
5. Guest Networks and creating Multiple Networks (more than one Wi-Fi to connect to)
6. Timed Access (control when it is switched on & off, handy for controlling children & place of business when closed)
7. Workplace Wi-Fi
8. MAC address filtering
9. Parental Control
10. Static IP address and address reservation
11. How to turn your Wi-Fi off or on
12. Purchasing your own router for additional features

9.1. ACCESSING YOUR ROUTER'S ADMIN SETTINGS

Most router settings can be accessed by typing directly into the address bar of any internet browser an IP address e.g., 123.456.7.9. **This is your router's internal IP address to access your router's admin settings.** Please consult your user manual, or contact your Internet provider for your IP address. The address bar is where you see a web address starting http://. Internet browsers have been mentioned in banking in the previous chapter.

Here is an example the access address of some routers I have used in the past.
Fig-9.1 The router's instructions were to type in an IP address.
Fig-9.2 The router's instructions were to type the following URL www.netgearlogin.net
Fig-9.1 & Fig-9.2

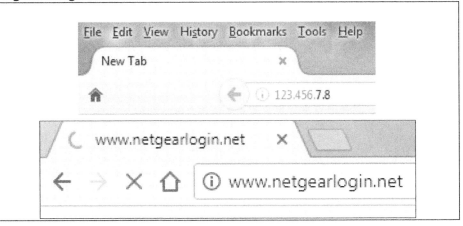

Next, you will be presented with the login page – See Fig 9.3

Fig-9.3

Please sign in

http://www.routerlogin.net requires a username and password.

Your connection to this site is not secure

Username: admin

Password: ********

Sign in   Cancel

After you log in, you will usually have a home page of some sort (see fig 9.4 & 9.5).

Fig-9.4

Fig-9.5

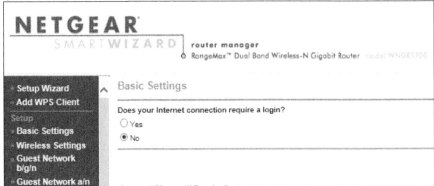

9.2. CHANGE YOUR ROUTER PASSWORD
Routers have two passwords:
1. To access the **admin settings** – known as the router password.
2. To access the **Wi-Fi – known** as the Wi-Fi password.

Your Wi-Fi password is probably not the same password as your admin login, nor should it be.

Often the default Admin and Wi-Fi passwords will either be:
- On the underside of the device.
- On some sort of sticky labels supplied.
- Contained within the instructions.

If the instructions are vague or you don't have any, contact your ISP for free help.

If you have your own purchased router, you can probably find the default details ONLINE.

If you have previously set your own passwords but can't recall them then, your only options are to contact support, or pay for a tech support.

You might be thinking 'Why bother changing your routers passwords?' In our current world, barely a month goes by without some company hitting the news for being hacked. Banks, retailers, phone companies etc. Remember "RELY ON NO-ONE".

With early broadband, you needed a modem and a router; your internet supplier would supply the modem and you purchased your own router. Initially the router needed configuring (setting up) and the default Admin and Wi-Fi passwords were all the same, requiring you to select your own; imagine a world where all bank cards were issued with the same PIN 1111.

Nowadays, the modem and router tend to be combined into one unit and your Wi-Fi password is unique when it is supplied to you. For all we know, router manufacturers may store all the default Wi-Fi passwords somewhere. After all, banks have to store your PIN somewhere, otherwise the ATMs or POS terminal at the till won't know if you are using the correct PIN. Think about it; if you forgot your PIN and ask your bank for a new one, it will arrive in the post; when you use the card for the first time, your location has to connect to the bank to verify your PIN.

So, if your router's default Admin and Wi-Fi passwords are stored somewhere, what happens if they are hacked; after all, it seems in today's world, no-one is safe.

Admin password – This is the password used to connect to the router for admin settings.
1. Don't use the default password.
2. It should be a Tier-4 password (see chapter 8 Passwords).
3. It does not need to be disclosed to *all* family members.
4. Best to access the router from a wired connection only, thus no exposure if any mobile device (including tablets) is lost or stolen.
5. If you don't have any wired computers, it is best to stick to one device for access, e.g., just one laptop.
    a. Do not forget, many laptops have an Ethernet port for cable connections.
    b. Ethernet ports are a bigger version of a landline phone cable port.

Wi-Fi password – This is the password used to connect to the router for Internet access.
1. Don't use the default password.
2. Don't use the same password as your admin password.
3. Always change your password if anyone loses a device that was connected to your router. Any computer tech can obtain your saved

passwords from your device. Even if they don't want to hack you, they can use your Internet link up to download illegal content or simply use up your data allowance if you have one.

CHANGING ADMIN PASSWORDS

To change your passwords;

1) Browse your menu settings; you are looking for admin, advanced settings, security, or simply set password etc. Examples below;

Fig-9.6

Fig-9.7

Fig-9.8

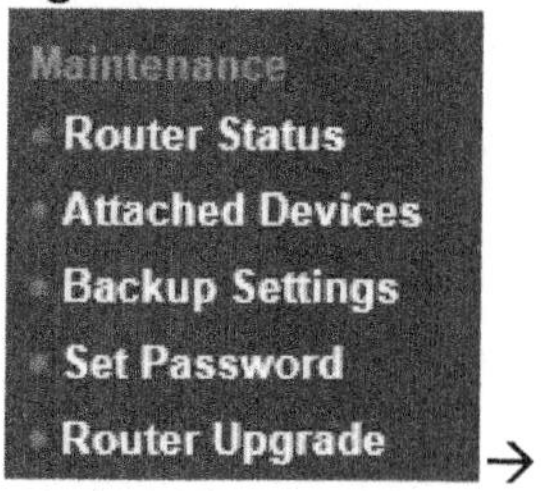

Maintenance
- Router Status
- Attached Devices
- Backup Settings
- Set Password
- Router Upgrade →

Fig-9.9

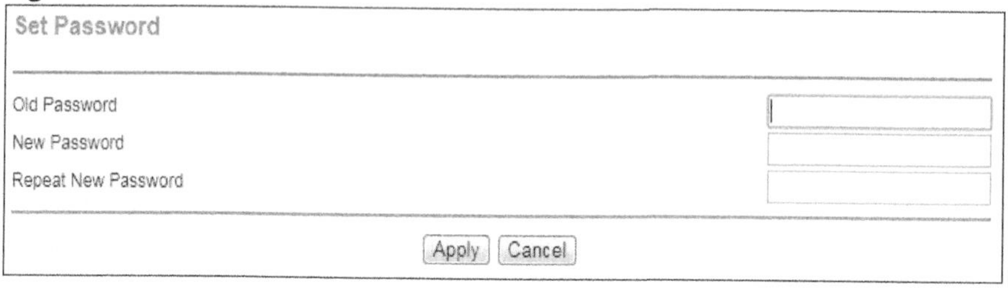

Set Password	
Old Password	
New Password	
Repeat New Password	

Apply   Cancel

Before you apply the changes, write the new and old passwords down; once you have applied it, some routers log you out for you to re-log back in. There is usually no going back or recovery. Some routers will have a factory-reset button, others do not. Once you have confirmed the new password is accepted, destroy the piece of paper.

CHANGING Wi-Fi PASSWORD

Again, browse your routers menus; you are usually looking for the word 'wireless'.

Fig-9.10

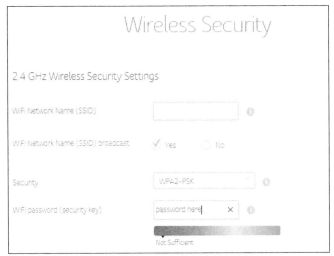

Fig-9.11

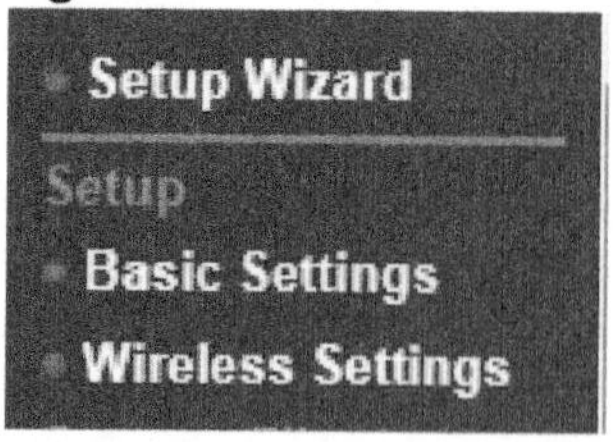

Fig-9.12

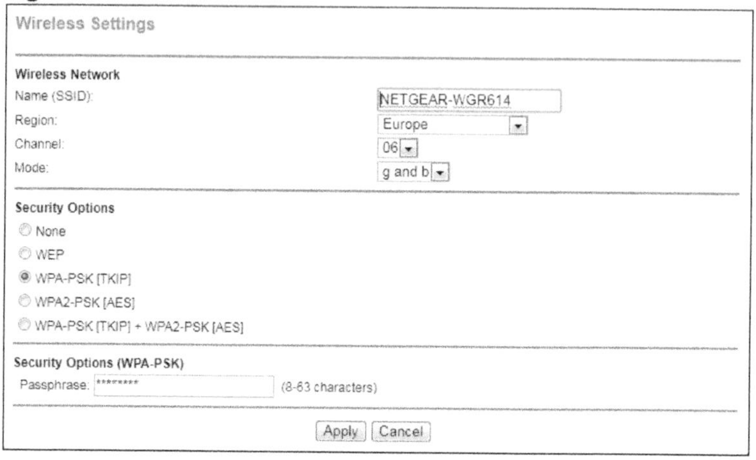

TIP: some routers auto-update the password on each device that is currently connected to the Wi-Fi, so you don't have to go around changing all the passwords on every device.

TIP: Before applying a new password, turn on all of your devices that use Wi-Fi and connect them to the Wi-Fi; phones, tablets, laptops, iPods, TV streaming devices, Amazon devices, Games consoles, smart TV/DVD/fridges/device for your electric/room lights (if you have such gadgets). If your router auto-updates all currently connected devices, this will save you a job later.

9.3. ROUTER SECURITY

All routers have various security settings, from none too high. WEP is the lowest level of security and should be avoided. You should always pick the higher levels of security. Some of your devices with Wi-Fi around the home may not connect to the highest security setting on your router, so you may need to select a level within the middle range. I recommend that you use one of the settings that commence WPA.

The security options can usually be found in the wireless setting where you change the Wi-Fi password.

Fig-9.13

9.4.1. SSID

SSID is the name of your Wi-Fi when your device searches for Wi-Fi. You can control the router's name seen to others or when you search for it yourself. (Service Set Identifier).

Fig-9.14

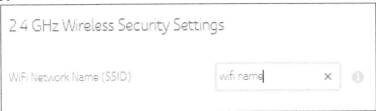

Imagine the internet as a big room with many windows. When you are connected to it, you are poking your head through the window. You can see people, people can see you with your router's name above your head; similar to an aeroplane SWALK signature on a radar screen, like something we see in movies for example; When air traffic controllers monitor planes on their radar, each plane on the screen has an I.D. code next to it, this code is transmitted by the plane and is called an SWALK I.D.

Don't use an SSID that can identify you and your household e.g., "Smith Family", "John's Wi-Fi", "Scotland" if you are the only Scottish family in the street, everyone will know it is yours. You want to remain anonymous, so pick a non-descriptive name.

You could leave it at the default SSID "Sky 5678" or "Virgin 1234" as they don't identify you, but if ever your internet provider is hacked, someone could find the router you were issued and obtain your router's ID and issued password.

You will more than likely click on a phishing link accidentally, you should not discount being hacked - why take the chance for a simple name change. If your router's manufacturer is compromised and 50% of people have not changed their default SSID and passwords, the criminals will go after the easy targets.

9.4.2. SSID BROADCAST

Now imagine your router's ID is like a number plate on your car. When you go out driving, people can see you and see your number plate. This is similar to an SSID broadcast.

Fig-9.15

You can switch off your SSID broadcast. Similarly, if a plane switches off its SWALK - the radar can still detect the aircraft, but it cannot be identified.

There is a downside; when you wish to connect a new device, your network will not be visible to the new device, meaning you can either:
> Manually enter the details on the new device.
> Temporarily switch back on your SSID broadcast to connect the new device, then switch off your SSID again.

Occasionally, some devices may not connect properly when the SSID broadcast is off. We had an issue with our TV provider, it would not connect while our SSID was turned off. If this occurs, consult a tech support, refer to the device support, or leave the SSID on; hence the recommendation of renaming the SSID to something that does not identify you. An alternative solution is to connect the TV box via an Ethernet cable, which is actually more reliable and faster.

It is not essential to turn off the SSID broadcast. It is just something extra to protect you. Probably more useful in shared accommodation, such as a student housing or a block of flats. It is more reliable if connecting only a few devices.

Changing the default SSID, admin login password and Wi-Fi password to good passwords is an excellent start.

Your Wi-Fi Password, Router security, SSID & SSID broadcast are normally in the same section on the router.

9.5. GUEST NETWORKS and MULTIPLE NETWORKS

Most routers have multiple networks, meaning you can broadcast more than Wi-Fi (or SSID).

Some have 2G and 5G are on separate networks, meaning you can separate what everyone connects to if you wish. 5G is faster and better for video, but it has a smaller range. 2G tends to be more stable, reliable with a better range, but slower. Some Routers automatically control the 2G and 5G connection depending on the device and its location in relation to the router.

The main issue to be aware of is anyone using your main Wi-Fi has what's called *administrator privileges*, meaning they POTENTIALLY have access to your router settings (assuming they have your admin password, which is why your admin password should not be the same as your Wi-Fi password).

Most routers also have what's called a 'GUEST NETWORK'. Your standard network (SSID) that you connect to will have administrator privileges, meaning anyone connected to the standard network has access the router settings; hence why it should be a Tier-4 password.

The guest network does not allow administrator privileges and so, anyone using it cannot access your router settings. There is no reason why guests should have such access. **REFER;** back to the *'the tradesman scam'* in chapter 1, para 1.14; if Bella had the *'guest network'* activated and displayed on the chalk board, the fraudster would not have been able to connect to the other devices on the network and install *'SPYWARE'* and thus not obtain her banking login's.

Imagine any one of your visitors has their phone lost or stolen and your Wi-Fi password is saved on it, any criminal could gain access but if they only have a guest network password, the damage any fraudster can do is severely limited.

You can even go further than that.
I change my guest network password every time it is used:
1. After every party.
2. After a family member stays for a weekend.
3. After a friend has popped in for a brief visit.
4. Use a different password to your main network.

A cyber-crime police inspector confirmed that whilst it is hard and rare to crack a mobile phone with a PIN, the software does exist to crack phones. If a criminal has the technology to crack phones, I have no doubt that they have the ability to gain access to your saved Wi-Fi, its location and password. Also, it only takes one rogue employee who works for a phone manufacturer who is desperate for money and targeted by criminals to supply the codes to crack phones en mass.

I change the guest network password within 24 hours; hence it is ready for the next visitor and I keep my system protected. Thus, if any guest loses their device, or it is stolen and subsequently hacked, you are not at risk. Neither is your business customer/client data, nor your banking or personal details at home. Important advice if you work from home with confidential files and client/customer/patient personal data.

Fig-9.16

If you change the guest network Wi-Fi password regularly, a Tier-1 password will be sufficient. So, you don't recycle words, use an online random word generator.

If everyone in your household connects their mobile device to the guest Wi-Fi, then if anyone's device is lost or stolen, your main Wi-Fi is safe and you could change the guest Wi-Fi password to remain safe.

You might think this is all unnecessary, but with most of us using online banking and shopping platforms, if your network is hacked, fraudsters can easily monitor your online activity until they obtain your financial details.

9.6. TIMED ACCESS

Many routers contain a setting for timed access, meaning you can program when the Wi-Fi will be on or off. This can be helpful to prevent young children from watching Netflix, or playing games when they should be sleeping.

For example, when I have a family BBQ, I pre-program the guest Wi-Fi to switch off around the time I plan to go to bed, thus if anyone's phone is lost or stolen after my guests have left, I am not left unprotected.

Fig-9.17

Fig-9.18

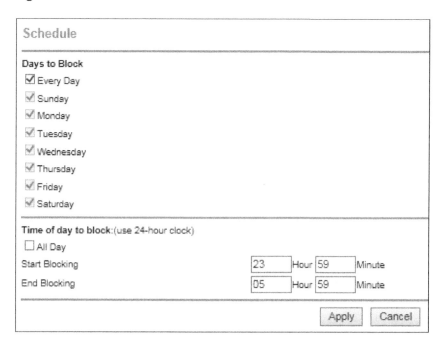

TIP: If the house is left unattended overnight or during a holiday, turn off the Wi-Fi altogether.

9.7. WORKPLACE Wi-Fi

When a member of staff leaves who has had access to the safe, or other security codes, the codes are changed. Now we have Wi-Fi, more damage can be done; data is far more important to be kept safe, especially with the current Data Protection Regulations.

1. You wouldn't give all staff the keys to the safe so all staff should not have access to administrator privileges.
2. Only allow staff to use the Guest Network.
3. Change the Wi-Fi password every time a member of staff leaves.
4. Utilise the timed access to switch on the Wi-Fi during working hours only, so staff/ex-staff/fraudsters cannot access after-hours, or the weekend to download illegal content or have plenty of time to steal data. There is no need to leave your Wi-Fi on during non-business hours, doing so is like leaving the front door unlocked when you leave home.
5. Remember your Wi-Fi is the gatekeeper to your digital world.

I have heard on a radio documentary, how an ex-member of staff, parked outside after hours and used the Wi-Fi to buy illegal weapons. They could also use it for child pornography and or steel customer's/supplier's data to start their own business in competition with you.

Businesses are charged with keeping clients/customers data safe, plus these days your data is arguably more valuable, hence it is worth taking every precaution because the repercussions are high such as:
- Lost customers
- Poor feedback
- Regulator fines – If the Information Commissioners Office (ICO) deems you were negligent, or careless in protecting your digital data, the fine in the UK is up to 4% of your sales turnover.

9.8. MAC ADDRESS FILTERING (MAC Media Access Control)

Before we get onto *'MAC address'* filtering, let me explain what a *'MAC address'* is. A MAC address is an electronic serial number unique to each electronic device for the purposes of connecting to any network via cable or Wi-Fi. Globally, no two devices contain the same MAC address. All MAC address are hard-coded into the network card within each device and cannot be changed. A MAC address is a series of letter and number groups that are always presented in this format; for example, **AB:12:CD:34:EF:56.**

Everything capable of a network connection will have a MAC address: desktop computers, laptops, tablets, Kindle's, smartphones, smart TV's, satellite or cable TV, games consoles, iPod's, Amazon devices, chrome cast, devices to control items at home e.g., heating, lights etc. This list is not exhaustive.

MAC ADDRESS FILTERING broadly means you create a pre-approved Wi-Fi list. On your router, you create a list of all your devices that you want to permit to use your Wi-Fi; once you activate the list, any device not on the list will not be able to connect to your network. Put simply, when MAC address filtering is on, it makes your network a little harder to hack. More advanced hackers could penetrate it, meaning for the average home network it is not worth the hassle. Fraudsters like easy targets, so with MAC address filtering activated, you won't be such an easy target.

Before you think to yourself, why you should bother with this – please refer back to scam 1.14 in chapter 1. In that case study, if Bella had MAC Address Filtering enabled, the fraudster might not have been able to gain access to her Wi-Fi and install '*SPYWARE*' onto her device(s).

How to find your MAC address: the interface layout will look different on each make & model, so pictures won't be useful.
  a) Routers and some devices may have the MAC address printed on the device somewhere (underneath).
  b) Within your device setting somewhere for phones and tablets. Many phones also have its MAC address printed on its original box.
  c) Disconnect your device from the Wi-Fi and log into your router, there will be a section 'Attached devices' or 'Connected devices'. Re-attach your device and refresh the list. Most devices will be obvious from the name but some are not so obvious, hence disconnecting first.

Fig-9.19 – is an example list of connected devices.

Device name	MAC address	IP address	Connected
Home desktop	90:FB:A0:61:PL:F7	192.168.0.2	Ethernet
Laptop-1	A0:61:F7:UJ:98:H8	192.168.0.3	Wi-Fi 5G
MacBook-pro	F7:FC:A2:F5:DB:00	192.168.0.4	Wi-Fi 5G
Bob's-iPhone	D7:E8:2D:4C:6B:E8	192.168.0.5	Wi-Fi 5G
Ann's-iPad	5F:60:4A:0C:F9:C0	192.168.0.6	Wi-Fi 5G
Bill's-Galaxy-S8	E5:D9:FE:14:01:0A	192.168.0.7	Wi-Fi 5G
Cable-TV	AA:01:CC:02:DD:03	192.168.0.9	Wi-Fi 5G
Foxtel	99:ZZ:88:YY:77:XX	192.168.0.10	Wi-Fi 5G
unknown	A1:B2:C3:D4:E5:F6	192.168.0.11	Wi-Fi 5G
Smart-TV	6F:5E:4D:3C:2B:1A	192.168.0.13	Wi-Fi 5G

HOW TO USE MAC ADDRESS FILTERING: CONSULT YOUR MANUAL.

If the instructions are vague, or you don't have any, contact your ISP for free help. If you have your own purchased router, you can probably find the details online or contact a tech support person.

I cannot give you precise instructions on setting this up, as each router will vary. All I can give you are insights.

Before starting it may be helpful to write down the MAC address of each device. See above to find your MAC address for each device.

1. Connect all the devices you wish to be on your list.
2. Log into your router through your admin settings.
3. Go to your MAC address filtering area which usually within the security setting.
4. Usually there is an add device function, so you add each device.
   a. You may be able to populate your list from the connected devices.
5. Activate or turn on MAC address filtering.

Fig-9.20 – Typically you have MAC address filtering off or disabled whilst you add devices. This is also the default mode on all new Routers when they come out the box.

Connect all the devices you wish to be on your list to your Wi-Fi. Use the attached devices section to view all the connected devices.

Fig-9.21

Add each device to your MAC address pre-approved list.

Fig-9.22

Fig-9.20 Turn on your MAC address filtering

NOTE – how to add new devices to an already active MAC address filter: To add a new device to your pre-approved MAC address filter, you will need to:

- ✓ Disable MAC address filtering first.
- ✓ Add the device to the Wi-Fi.
- ✓ Add the device to your MAC address filter list.
- ✓ Re-activate the MAC address filter.

TIPS:

- ➢ Your MAC address filter will apply to the main network, not the guest Wi-Fi.
- ➢ If you have family and friends who use your Wi-Fi on a regular basis and you wish to use the MAC address filtering feature, it is recommended you have your household devices on the main network and use the guest Wi-Fi feature for all visitors.
- ➢ If your phone/device is lost or stolen, you can navigate to your MAC address-filtering feature, remove the lost/stolen device and reapply the MAC address filter.
  - ○ Although the lost/stolen device can no longer access the router whilst the MAC address filter on. I would recommend you still change the Wi-Fi password as well to cover yourself for anytime you deactivate the MAC address filter.
- ➢ Remember; often when you change the Wi-Fi password, any device currently connected is automatically updated, (depending on your router); this saves time updating each device when they want to reconnect to the network.

9.9. PARENTAL CONTROL

Some routers have a parental control section. If there is no parental control section, we can use other features to circumvent our requirements.

1. Connect all Children's devices to the Guest Network. At the very least you can turn off, or put the guest Wi-Fi on a timed access so they cannot use it when they should be sleeping or doing their homework. The benefit is it won't interrupt the adults using the Wi-Fi whilst the kids are locked out of the WI-FI.
2. There may be a 'block sites' section. You create a keyword list. You can also see that you can create trusted devices. A trusted device will not be blocked, thus again allowing adults to view websites that you

don't want your children to visit. It does require a static IP address (see Para 9.10 below).

Fig-9.23

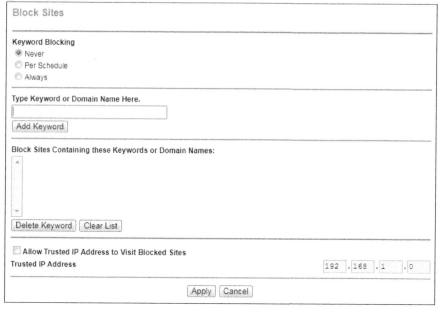

The advantages of not using parental control software are:
- ✓ Less software to slow down a computer/device, or use more battery power.
- ✓ Costing of licences for multiple devices.
- ✓ Children are resourceful, they may well get around the software.
- ✓ If they are on the guest Wi-Fi, they cannot access the router's settings.

A little perseverance to set it up is worthwhile.

9.10. STATIC IP ADDRESS / ADDRESS RESERVATION / IP RANGE

This section has little security value but may just assist with the parental control section.

All computers/devices are issued an IP whether they are connected via an Ethernet cable or Wi-Fi. Routers usually set the IP address to each device every time it connects, e.g., your phone when you return home. Whilst the IP address to the property never changes, the IP address in each device changes constantly; this is known as dynamic IP address.

A static IP address or address reservation is where we lock an IP to a specific device, so it never changes. Uses are:
- ✓ Setting a trusted device for permitted access through your block sites list.
- ✓ If you plug your printer into the router instead of a computer, known as a network printer; many printers have this capability. It is easier to share the printer with several computers.
- ✓ Remote access from one device to another e.g., in your living room on your laptop, while you wish to access the computer in the study/office.

IP RANGE

IP range does offer some security value. The IP range controls how many devices you permit to use your router thus reducing the risk of hacking, or simply any of your neighbours from hi-jacking your Wi-Fi which may slow your broad band service, or used for cyber-crime.

Many typical routers will issue an IP address commencing 192.168.0.1 or 192.168.1.0

The first IP is usually reserved for the router itself 192.168.0.1 so all your connected devices will start with
192.168.0.2
192.168.0.3 And so on.

The router will automatically have a default range. E.g.
- 192.168.0.2 to 192.168.0.10, will allow 9 devices to be connected.
- 192.168.0.2. to 192.168.0.25, will allow 24 devices to be connected.

Therefore, you can edit this section to decrease or increase the permitted devices depending on your household size and number of devices.

It is very easy to adjust these settings and it only takes a few minutes.

CASE STUDY: *Bill lives on his own but is very cautious. He has one phone, one tablet, one laptop and one desktop and a smart TV for streaming services with nothing else connected to Wi-Fi such as fridges, heating, smart lighting. Therefore, he wants to allow room on his router for a guest that pops round a coffee, so he sets its IP RANGE for 6-devices. His IP range would be 192.168.0.2 to 192.168.7. Bill is planning a birthday party, he already has his guest Wi-Fi set up but only has one available IP slot, knowing all his friends will want to access Wi-Fi to post pictures of the party on social media; he logs into his router and increases the IP RANGE accordingly. The following day, he reverts the IP range back to its original setting.*

Fig-9.24
Step-1 Address reservation start and IP range.

Fig-9.25

Advanced
- Wireless Settings
- Wireless Repeating Function
- Port Forwarding / Port Triggering
- WAN Setup
- LAN Setup

This router is referred to as LAN set-up.

Fig-9.26 Setting an IP range.

☑ Use Router as DHCP Server				
Starting IP Address	192	168	1	2
Ending IP Address	192	168	1	25

9.11. TURNING YOUR Wi-Fi ON or OFF

If your house is empty, i.e., when going on holiday, turn your Wi-Fi off. If a fraudster parks outside, attempting to gain access to your router, you would probably notice them after a while when you are home, but if you're away, who will challenge them? If the Wi-Fi is off, then no one can hack this. It can be done by either a button on the device, or within the admin settings. You can see here there is a disable each frequency. Alternatively, unplug from the wall.

Fig-9.27 you would tick the disable radio button and click save.

9.12. PURCHASING YOUR OWN ROUTER

With earlier versions of broadband, a modem and router were needed; your ISP supplied the modem and you bought your own router. Purchased routers tend to have more features. Common brands were Netgear, D-link, TP-link, Linksys, Asus. These days, modems and routers tend to be built into one device.

Your supplied router from your ISP may not have enough features, so you can still purchase an additional one. If you purchase your own, you still need the ISP's device supplied to plug into your phone line to obtain your IP address and internet connection. Thus, the router supplied by your ISP's will become the modem similar to early broadband. Your ISP's router will have a standalone modem function to facilitate this, then you can plug a third-party router into the router supplied by your ISP.

Fig-9.28

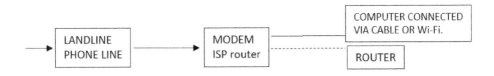

You cannot have two routers working simultaneously, hence the ISP router is put into modem-only mode. To apply this, you will need to enable your router's MODEM MODE; the internet connection will pass through the MODEM into your router for the Wi-Fi.

Fig-9.29

You can revert back to using just the one router supplied

Fig-9.30

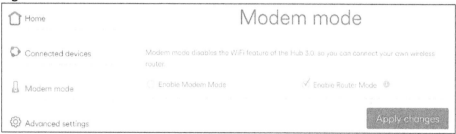

TIP: before you consider your router purchase
In the UK there are two versions; ADSL or DSL and they work with different types of phone lines e.g., British-Telecom/Virgin/AT&T/Century-Link. Consult your landline phone provider to find out which type will be compatible with your phone line.

Advantage: You have probably heard of Anti-virus and Internet security, which contains a firewall to prevent hackers. All routers by design are also a hardware (physical) firewall, by having a second router you can increase your firewall protection.

I suggest only purchasing a separate router for the features that suit your requirements and not if your only reason was a second hardware firewall. Having strong passwords and paid-for Internet Security is more important.

OTHER ROUTER SETTINGS

Some more advanced settings you can use:

1. You can restrict the admin login to one device only, meaning all other devices cannot login into admin settings.
2. IP address reservation – (known as DHCP) means you can save a particular IP address for some or all devices. This is handy if accessing remotely across your network.
3. Relay - with more than one router, one can be a relay to extend your Wi-Fi, often known as *'Wi-Fi repeating'*.

10. DOMAIN NAMES – USING DOMAIN NAMES TO ENHANCE PROTECTION

Free help is available from the domain register you purchase a domain from.

Using domain names to protect yourself further.

Chapter Sections
1. Domain name overview.
2. How to use the domain to protect yourself.
3. What if one of your online accounts is hacked.
4. Understanding the difference between a Mailbox and an Alias.
5. Purchasing a domain name.
6. Setting up the email
   a. Email forwarding – cheaper option.
   b. Email hosting – better services – costs can be inexpensive.

10.1 DOMAIN NAME OVERVIEW

My first email in the mid '90's predated the existence of Google with Gmail and Hotmail. I foresaw the logistical nightmare of notifying all my contacts with a new email address, let alone other things I didn't predict such as needing it for online shopping accounts etc. Therefore, I bought a domain name for personal use and one for business use. This turned out to be an excellent decision since my internet supplier was later rebranded twice, resulting in the email address changing on each occasion.

The same would apply if you changed internet service providers such as Sky, Virgin, BT and you use their email structure; i.e., sky.com, virginmedia.com, btinternet.com or btconnect.com. Having to inform all your contacts and notify all your logins that you have changed is most tedious. If you change provider but want to keep your previous email, you will be charged for this and can be held to ransom on the price.

A 'domain name' comes after the 'www.'within a web address, or after the '@' symbol in an email address.

Example of domains are; example.com, example.co.uk, example.net, example.org, example.info, example.tv, example.biz, example.uk etc. In fact, the list of suffices (.com, .co.uk, .uk etc.) is now almost endless.

For this demonstration purpose, the domain I will use is 'example.com'. If I were creating a web site, it would be www.example.com. But when you buy a domain name, you don't have to create a website. To create an email address we simply add anything@ in front of your domain: e.g. info@example.com, admin@example.com, sales@example.com, john@example.com, john1@example.com etc. You are only limited by your imagination, e.g. 'dizzybird@example.com', 'pussinboots@example.com'.

Tips on creating your own email address:
1. You can have one for each family member
2. Using a decimal point between the names will reduce the spam received; e.g., john.doe@example.com
3. Using numbers in the email will reduce the spam received; e.g., johndoe1@example.com or even john.doe1@example.com

10.2 HOW USING A DOMAIN NAME FOR PROTECTION
If you are ever hacked, comprised, have a stalker or just receive too much spam, you can simply create new email addresses and delete others at will. New ones are often up and running within minutes. This is where we can be really clever to give you a lot of protection.

CASE STUDY: *most people have only one email address. Hence it is used for all your username logins. From time-to-time companies are hacked and your contact details are stolen, resulting in receiving spam and fraudulent emails to our inbox. The fraudsters are clever at making fraudulent emails look genuine; hence it is increasingly harder to distinguish which ones are genuine.*

Imagine you have a separate email for a sensitive item e.g., Amazon which would be amazon@example.com. The only company that knows of the existence of this email is Amazon - therefore if you receive emails concerning your Amazon account to your new Amazon email, the chances are it will be genuine. After you create your new separate email and change your username login to your new email and you receive emails concerning your Amazon account to your previous email, there is a good chance it is fraudulent. It is not a fool proof method, but it increases your chances of detecting the fraudulent emails.

E.g., your main email is 'john@example.com', if you receive and email about your Amazon account suggesting there is an issue, you know it is a fake email because they did not email your new Amazon email 'amazon@example.com'.

My idea is to create a separate email for each important login as your username.

- o amazon@example.com
- o ebay@example.com
- o paypal@example.com
- o netflix@example.com

You could create a new email address for every login account you have. Although this is possible, it could be quite cumbersome. But you could do it gradually, or apply the principle to all new online accounts you set up.

TIP: if you receive an email about eBay, Netflix or Amazon that is addressed to your main email instead of the relevant email, you know it will be fake.

You might be thinking, "if I have all these emails addresses, do I have to check all these email address for mail" or, "I can't be bothered to check all these email addresses". You don't have to. You can channel it all into one email, or your existing email address so it is altogether in one inbox.

TIP: don't use the same password for each account. If one of your accounts is hacked such as amazon, it doesn't take a genius to think "I see they use a domain with amazon in the front, I wonder if they used the same system for PayPal, I will try paypal@example.com with the same password and see if I am successful."

This whole idea is designed to help distinguish fraudulent emails from the genuine ones, thus greatly reducing the risk of you becoming a victim of a phishing attack.

Technically, you don't need to purchase a domain name to have the same effect. You can create additional email addresses with your chosen provider such as Gmail. You could adopt the new protocols with no additional costs.

CASE STUDY: *your primary or only email is bob@gmail.com. You then create bob.paypal@gmail.com, bob.amazon@gmail.com, bob.netflix@gmail.com. You follow this pattern – of course assuming that these email addresses with Gmail have not been taken. You can adopt the same principle with hotmail.com or any other email provider.*

As above, don't think by having all these different emails that you have to check them all. Most email providers have a forwarding function so that you can forward all your new email addresses to your original email address i.e.: bob@gmail.com. Alternatively, Gmail will allow you to access other email address in one location.

The advantage of purchasing a domain is your choice of email addresses are unlimited and guaranteed to be available because you own the domain.

10.3 IF YOUR ONLINE ACCOUNT IS HACKED
1. Don't make a rash decision – you may be tempted to delete your account, so don't.
    a. If you delete an online account e.g., eBay, PayPal or a shopping site etc. you will lose your purchase history.
    b. You never know when you will need your purchase history as proof of purchase for any insurance claim or tax receipts.
2. Obviously, the first thing is to change your password to a temporary one, as the plan is to change it again.
3. Log into your domain hosting company, (we will cover a domain hosting company in para-10.6) and create a new email e.g., amazon2@example.com (we will cover creating new email addresses soon).
4. Wait about 5mins then test the new email amazon2@example.com by sending yourself an email.
    a. This is important because, the email has to be working as many companies ask you to confirm any changes to your account.

b. Sending yourself emails is also a good way of backing up information and files, as a copy is in the Sent items folder, as well as the Inbox.

5. Log back into the hacked account and within the Settings; change your user name to the new email address you just created. (PayPal has an unorthodox method for changing your Username; see Chapter 11 for instructions).

6. You may need to confirm the new email, hence why we tested it in item-4 above.

7. For good measure, I recommend changing the password a second time.

8. **This results in** completely new login credentials, but you have preserved your purchase history.

Because you can create an unlimited number of email addresses, if an online account is hacked you can change the Username with a new email address very quickly in order to keep your account secure, especially when the password is changed as well.

This outlines the principle of using domain names as a tool to compartmentalise and create multiple email addresses for use with various online accounts.

Why is this worth considering?

CASE STUDY: *We are guilty of using the same email username and password for multiple logins. Imagine your eBay account is hacked, then the fraudster tries the same email and password on PayPal to find that they are successful, resulting in fraudulent activity on your debit or credit card. This happened to me.*

By using a different email address for various login Usernames, with different passwords, you are reducing your risk of being hacked. Recall my first sentence in this book; "more crime will be committed online and statistically you are more likely to be a victim of cyber-crime than physical crime."
It may sound far-fetched but it happens to more people every day. At least if one of your online accounts is hacked, it will be limited to one account and the fraudsters will not be able to gain access to others.

10.4 UNDERSTANDING MAILBOXES AND ALIASES

Your current email provider will provide extra help required, normally free of charge.

Before we start, we need to understand the differences between a mailbox and an alias.

- A **mailbox** is where you can actually receive, view and send emails.
- An **alias** is a fictitious email that piggy backs on your main email.
    - ○ You cannot send mail from an alias, only receive.
    - ○ It will be received in the inbox of the primary email.
    - ○ You can have multiple alias email addresses feeding into your main mailbox.
    - ○ In some cases, you may be able to access the incoming mail in an alias separately; similar to its own inbox. This will depend on your email provider and subject to change.

I have used aliases and they are very handy for using temporarily for something specific; e.g., obtaining a quote from a company (say car insurance) but don't wish to receive future advertising emails; simply delete the alias when no longer required.

Aliases have genuine applications by helping individuals manage and sort their emails

E.g.: Your email is bob@example.com and you would like to compartmentalise your emails but you don't want the hassle of logging into more than one email inbox to view your mail, you can create an alias e.g. bobsales@example.com, so all the mail will be delivered to your *primary* mailbox bob@example.com, thus you can view emails sent to both bob@ and bobsales@ in one inbox in your email. An alias won't have a mailbox of its own, so you cannot send mail from bobsales@example.com. All outgoing mail will originate from just bob@example.com

Some email suppliers do permit alias email addresses, or you may need an advanced account which may have a small fee to do so.

You can also use the email rules or filters (see chapter-13) so all your incoming emails to the alias email address 'bobsales@' are either copied, or moved into its own folder, resulting in your emails being organised automatically.

10.5 PURCHASING YOUR DOMAIN NAME

Don't worry; free assistance is available from companies that sell domain names. Don't be discouraged, the costs aren't necessarily expensive.

Before we get started, we need to buy a domain name. There are many companies that sell domain names known, as *'domain registrars'*. Once you have bought a domain name, you are known as the *registrant and* that domain is yours for the period of time you have purchased.

A domain purchase is <u>not</u> an outright purchase; you are buying the right to use it for a fixed period of time. When it expires you need to pay for the domain again. Options normally range from 1-10 year plans. The longer the period selected, the bigger the discount. Feel free to try shorter periods first. <u>When the renewal time comes, you are always given first refusal</u> so there is no need to panic; often you are also given a grace period e.g., 30 days during which it is not publicly relisted.

Cheap domains can be bought for as little as £10 for one year. Generally I renew my domain every 5-years at a time - costing £50, which for £10 a year I find to be very reasonable.

Tips for domain purchases:
1. Shop around, prices vary.
2. Pick something short; over time, you will type it a lot.
3. Initials tend to be cheaper.
   a. Unless your initials match an existing company e.g., Brian Tabb (BT) is the same as British Telecom.
   b. Pick something that means something to you.

Some domain registrars I have come across in the past are:

www.names.co.uk
www.easily.co.uk
www.123reg.com
www.1&1.com
www.dominit.com
www.godaddy.com

There are hundreds more globally.

10.6 SETTING UP YOUR EMAIL
Your domain registrar provider will supply any help required free of charge.

Options
Option-1 Email forwarding: You forward any of your new emails to your existing mailbox e.g., Gmail.
- I used this method myself for years before upgrading to Email hosting.

Option-2 Email hosting. This is a pay for service.
- Create as many mailbox accounts as you need.
- Create as many alias emails as you need.
- Both of these options greatly assist with using the domain name for protection.

If the registrar that you bought your domain from does not supply the service or mailbox size you desire, you can move your domain name to another registrar. You are not restricted to the hosting company with whom you bought the domain. You can purchase from a cheaper company and transfer the domain to a company who supplies a better or cheaper service.

To do this you have to change the DNS setting so the domain is parked in a new location.
1- Contact your new registrar for help and settings that are required.
2- Contact the existing registrar on how to change the settings so your domain is moved to the new registrar.

The variation within the different registrars globally is too vast for this book and subject to change, hence when the need arises to move registrars, speak to both companies and they will guide your through the process from start to finish, usually free of charge.

A key issue for assessing which company would be suitable for you is the mailbox size and price for that size. E.g., many companies offer as part of their package 15GB or 30GB of space for your emails, whilst other providers offer only 2GB.
As more companies want you to opt out of paper billing and paper statements, these will be supplied via email, therefore your need for online space will

grow. If you conduct a lot of your personal, or business correspondence via email, you may find a mailbox of 2GB is filled quickly; when full, incoming mail bounces back to the sender as *undeliverable*, but you, the recipient, could be none the wiser that your mailbox is full, resulting in urgent or important emails being missed.

10.6a OPTION 1 - EMAIL FORWARDING
With email forwarding, you don't pay for any email hosting; hence once you have bought the domain name, there are no further costs. As you are not paying for a hosting service this means it won't have a mailbox, so you cannot actually receive any emails to this account, nor can you send mail from your domain. You have to forward all incoming mail to an existing email with all outgoing mail being sent from your existing mailbox.

How to receive emails for your new domain to your existing email address; most domain registrar providers allow a free email-forwarding service (your domain provider will help you with this).

How this works:
- Assume the domain 'example.com' has been bought and you wish to use johndoe@example.com - this is an 'alias' because it doesn't have a mailbox that can collect email.
- Assume your existing email and mailbox currently is, for example; johndoe@gmail.com;
- Log into your registrars account where you bought 'example.com' and access the email forwarding settings and enter the email you with forward your email to, in this case it is johndoe@gmail.com;
- If you cannot find the email forwarding section, your domain provider will help you with this.

Fig-10.1 – example of mail forwarding to your existing email address

Because you are not paying for mailboxes, you can create as many aliases as we such as:
e.g., one for each member of the family.
johndoe@example.com
janedoe@example.com
joebloggs@example.com

Once you have created other aliases, you need to forward them to a genuine mailbox. You have the choice to send them:
- All to one mail box e.g., johndoe@gmail.com **(See Fig-10.2)**
- Each alias is forwarded to a separate email **(See Fig-10.3)**

Fig-10.2 – example of an alias email for each family member, forwarded to one primary email address.

(Fig-10.2) Here the setup is 3 email aliases being forwarded to one mailbox. You will receive mail sent to all 3 aliases in your family: John, Jane, Joe and into just one mailbox.
johndoe@example.com forwarded to johndoe@gmail.com
janedoe@example.com forwarded to johndoe@gmail.com
joebloggs@example.com forwarded to johndoe@gmail.com

Fig-10.3– example of an alias email for each family member, forwarded their own email address.

(Fig-10.3) Alternatively, if everyone in the family already has their own email address, you can set each alias to go to separate mailboxes.
johndoe@example.com forwarded to johndoe@gmail.com
janedoe@example.com forwarded to janedoe@hotmail.com
joebloggs@example.com forwarded to joeb@outlook.com

Once either method is set up you can continue to collect your emails through your normal method.

Email forwarding is fine for your online shopping logins where you only need to receive mail. My family operated like this for 20 years and it really keeps costs to a minimum.

CATCH ALL - You will have noticed there is something all the 'catch all'.
The catch-all section means *anything@example.com* will be forwarded to your mailbox johndoe@gmail.com; 'anything@' means you put literally anything in front the @ symbol, such as:
- mail@
- info@
- sales@
- spam@
- 123@
- 456@

This means if you wish to use the catch-all feature, you won't need to set up the email forwarding for each of the aliases as in Fig 10.2 & 10.3. This is fine if you intend to create many aliases to be sent to the one mail mailbox. Spam is often sent to *info@example.com,* *sales@example.com,* *admin@example.com*, therefore, I suggest not using the catch-all feature.

SOLUTION FOR SPAM

Entering into the 'catch all forwarding section' an email that either:

- Does not exist.
- An old email you do not care about.
- A spam collection email.
    - Most email providers have a good 'spam, phishing and fraud' filters which catch most emails, they are not perfect and learn as spammers change their tactics.
    - Most email providers have a designated email address that you can you forward suspicious emails to. It often appears as phishing@ or spam@. E.g., if your email is Gmail, it may look something like phishing@gmail.com or spam@gmail.com. If your email provider is Hotmail, it may look something like phishing@hotmail.com or spam@hotmail.com. Always check with your email provider if they have a spam and phishing email to forward suspicious emails. The more suspicious emails they collect, the better their systems become at providing everyone better protection.

By setting the catch-all to something other than your own email, any other mail that does not match the ones you created, will be sent to either the fictitious email and bounce back to the original spam sender, or be forwarded onto a spam filter.

Fig-10.4 – Here I have changed the catch-all to spam@gmail.com to catch all the fraud/spam and so only the emails aliases you create are sent into your genuine email.

Obviously, emails can still be sent directly to your normal email as well (Gmail in this case), nothing has changed here.

WHAT IF I CHANGE MY PRIMARY EMAIL SUPPLIER?

If you have used your domain for all your username logins and you decide to change your email, say, from 'Gmail' to 'Hotmail', all that has to be done is to log into the domain holding company, access the email forwarding settings and change the email forwarding from the current email address **Fig 10.4**, to the new email address **Fig 10.5**.

Fig-10.4 - Before

Fig-10.5 - After

DISADVANTAGE OF EMAIL FORWARDING

There is a drawback of just using mail forwarding, you cannot send mail from your new domain <u>yet</u>. Your purchased domain does not have any mailbox of its own which is why you cannot send mail from your new domain-example.com. You can only send emails from your original email account. If you don't send many emails, this may not be a concern.

Sometimes when you are looking for a refund on goods or services, for your protection the retailer or service provider will request that you send an email from the registered email on the account. You then have to explain how john.doe@example.com is an alias and you cannot send emails from it; you may be asked to provide other details to prove the account is yours.

BUT THERE IS A SOLUTION - EMAIL HOSTING.

10.6b OPTION 2 - EMAIL HOSTING
YOUR DOMAIN REGISTRAR PROVIDER WILL SUPPLY ANY HELP REQUIRED FREE OF CHARGE

If you prefer to actually send/receive your emails with their own mailbox, this will require email hosting. This service has a running cost, but they are very reasonable. No matter how many email mailboxes you wish to create, you can still choose to elect to receive all or some of them into one mailbox.

You can choose to have either:
1. One mailbox john@example.com with all your other emails as aliases that feed into one mailbox, similar to the mail forwarding; i.e., from the example above amazon@, paypal1@, netflix@, eBay@ etc. all feed into john@example.com. **(see Fig 10.7 shows a list of aliases created)**
   a. You will be able to send mail from john@example.com, but you won't be able to mail from the aliases.
   b. The advantage of the aliases is they cannot be hacked; they do not have a mailbox or password of their own, so no location to hack.
   c. Disadvantage of Aliases is similar to using the email forwarding in 9.6a; emails cannot be sent from the aliases, only john@example.com. In the event of chasing a refund this may pose as an issue. But the most important part of the email for security is the domain itself '@example.com'.
2. Create a mailbox for each email.
   a. Each mailbox can be accessed either separately, or all in one place.
   b. Each mailbox can have its own password if you wish, for other family members.
   c. You can send emails from each mailbox, e.g., if you want to email PayPal, you can send an email from your paypal@example.com to PayPal. This has added security for PayPal as the email is coming from the registered account.
   d. **Fig-10.8 & Fig-10.9** show how each mailbox has it is own mailbox, as well as copied to johndoe@example.com so they can be all viewed in one place.
   e. Your domain registrar provider will supply any help required.

Fig-10.6 – a list of created mailboxes

Name	Address	Recipients
john doe	johndoe@example.com	1
jane doe	jane@example.com	1
child 1	child1@example.com	1
paypal1	paypal1@example.com	2
paypal2	paypal2@example.com	2
sky	sky@example.com	2
netflix	netflix@example.com	2
ebay	ebay@example.com	2
amazon	amazon@example.com	2

Fig-10.7 –you can see that each mailbox is sent to itself and copied to your main email johndoe@example.com.

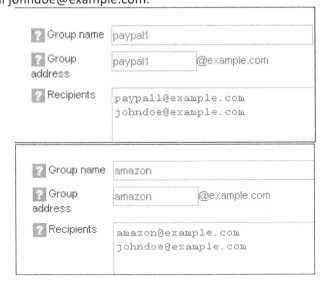

108

Fig-10.8

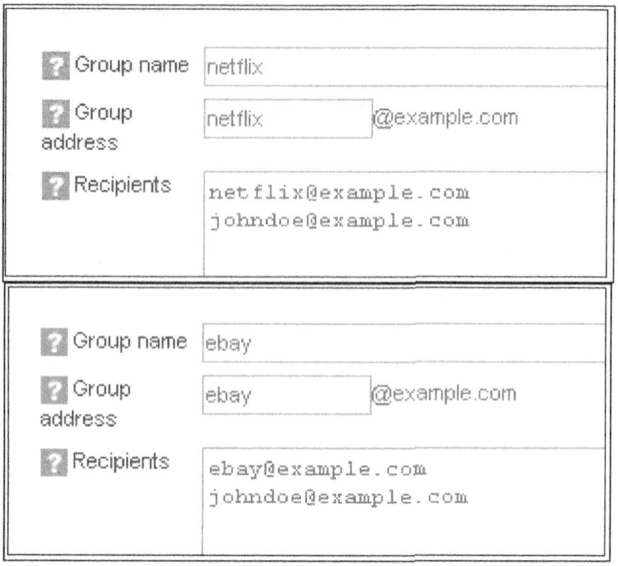

TIP: if you are looking for a specific email, you can go to the separate account e.g., Netflix, thus have an easier task finding the email you want because you are searching within a smaller list.

EMAIL HOSTING COSTS

Domain companies charge for email hosting so you need to do a little research before you engage. Companies either charge:

1. Per-domain name where you can have as many mailboxes and emails addresses as you like.
2. Per mailbox. E.g., you have three mailboxes, john.doe@example.com, jane.doe@example.com and joe.bloggs@example.com hence will pay three fees.
   a. This is only a good option if you only need one mailbox.

TIP: if you want to create many mailboxes, look for package deals.

Finally, if you own a business, having a domain name with email hosting appears more professional, as well as keeping your personal and business compartmentalised, it is very useful if you cease trading or sell the business.

EMAIL ADDRESS TIP: Some people like to use numbers in their email address. Some people use the year of their birth. Plus, when we create some online accounts, we are asked to create a user name or screen name. Many people include a 2-digit number year of birth too.

Junk mail (spam) is often generated by computer Algorithms, therefore, using numbers can be a good idea to combat spam, using your year of birth can be dangerous.

Hackers, frequently hack retailers and institutions to obtain customers' details, your details. When they obtain your details, they will attempt gain other details. The problem is if you use your year of birth in your email, you have given the fraudster one third of your date of birth (DOB). If the fraudster now sees any happy birthday wishes on any social media platform, they will now have your full DOB.

11. CHANGING YOUR PAYPAL USERNAME

Many online accounts permit you to change your username login, but some do not. PayPal does but it is not a straightforward process.

IF YOUR PayPal IS HACKED
- ✓ Don't make a rash decision, you may be tempted to delete your account.
- ✓ In section 10.3 we covered why you shouldn't rush to delete your account.
- ✓ PayPal is important as it provides, proof of purchase for many shopping sites.
- ✓ We can add a second email address as a second username to login.
- ✓ Once added, you can make the new email your primary email. Your original email becomes the secondary email username.
- ✓ Once the new email address is set to the primary username, you can delete the secondary email, (your original one).
- ✓ For good measure, change the password a second time.
- ✓ Result: Completely new login credentials, but you have preserved your purchase history.

Chapter 12 also provides additional tactics to engage to protect you further.

11.1 CHANGING YOUR PayPal USERNAME

TRAP: During the PayPal username change process, whilst two emails are registered you can log in with either one, hence the suggestion to use a temporary password until the new username login becomes the primary one and you have deleted the original username email.

INSTRUCTIONS ON CHANGING PayPal's EMAIL LOGIN Steps:
1) Settings.
2) Account.
3) Click the '+ sign' to the right of your email.
4) Add the new email address.
5) Click Update and confirm the new email.
6) Check your email & click on the link to confirm your email.

7) Once done, re-login into your PayPal. Next to the second email, click Update again.
8) Tick the box to make the new email the primary email.
9) Finally, back on the other screen, click Remove that is situated next to the Update button.

Step 1

Step 2

Step 3

Step 4

Step 5

Step 6

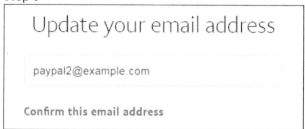

Step 7

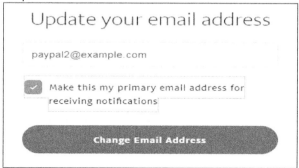

Step 8

Now any hacker doesn't know your new password or your email login – you are totally safe again.

12. ENHANCING YOUR PROTECTION THROUGH PAYPAL

You can add several cards or bank accounts to your PayPal wallet, giving you a variety of payment methods.
E.g.:
- o   Personal debit card.
- o   Personal credit card.
- o   Business credit card.

You can also register bank accounts, which is required if you sell, or wish to withdraw funds given to you.

CASE STUDY TRUE STORY: *KARL had his PayPal hacked and was fearful of the fraudsters obtained the full card details of all the other registered cards in the PayPal wallet, he then arranged for all registered cards to be cancelled. Obviously, those cards are now out of action until replacements arrive. If that is all of your bank/credit cards Karl no longer has access to funds.*

TIP: Do not register all of your bank cards; if your PayPal is hacked and you chose to cancel the linked cards, you still have access to funds.

Resulting from this I developed a new idea of having multiple PayPal accounts:
- o   I now have three PayPal account and only one card registered to each.
- o   They all have different passwords.
- o   I have a system that helps me remember them.
- o   When I change the card, I change the password.

Chapter Sections
1.   Using a domain name to provide further protection.
2.   Using free email to provide further protection.

12.1 USING A DOMAIN NAME TO PROVIDE FURTHER PROTECTION
Each account only has one credit card registered to it:
- o   paypal1@example.com has my personal credit card.
- o   paypal2@example.com has my business credit card.

o paypal3@example.com has my backup card; you may be hacked again and odds are when you are in a rush or at some other inconvenient time and don't have time to sort out a new PayPal login so you change your password and plan to sort it later by creating a new one paypal4@example.com, hence the spare one is useful.
o I no longer have registered any debit cards.

As an added measure you could include first 4-numbers, from your 16-digit card number used with each PayPal as part of your username or password. (15-digits for American Express Cards).

E.g., you register your credit card that commences 3742, so you create the email paypal3742@example.com, this is actually a great way of remember which card is registered with each PayPal account. Usually the first 4-digits identify the card issuer so it is unlikely to ever change.

You can use any set of 4-digits from the registered debit/credit card for part of the email. If a replacement card arrives with a different card number, or you wish to change the card you wish to use, you can create a new email address incorporating the new 4-digits of the replacement card.

If you use a set of 4-digits as part of your password, when you receive a replacement card, change the password as well.

You get the picture. If any of the accounts are hacked you can change your login username for it, even if you use the same password for each one. It will still be harder for the cyber-criminals to gain access because you are using a different login for each account.

12.2 USING FREE EMAIL TO PROVIDE FURTHER PROTECTION
You can still use this tactic with free email e.g., Gmail, Hotmail, outlook, or anything else. You could create such emails as:
o smith3742@gmail.com
o bloggs3742@hotmail.com
o paypalsmith3742@outlook.com

Or use the bank name in the email:
o smithamex@gmail.com

- o smithdiscover@gmail.com
- o smithbarclaycard@gmail.com

Or combine the two systems
- o smithamex3742@gmail.com
- o smithbarclaycard4929@gmail.com

Thus, you can create your own multiple email address for multiple PayPal usernames or anything else.

_____

13. TACTIC TO REDUCE SPAM & FRAUDULENT EMAILS

Also, for automatically organising your emails (I suggest that you are in front of your device with your emails open as you read this section, it will make more sense).
FREE HELP IS AVAILABLE FROM YOUR EMAIL PROVIDER.

Solution: Create Message Rules, or Filters. Message filters or rules are the same thing. Some email suppliers call them filters while others call them rules. Message filters/rules are a set of rules that emails will follow, resulting in automatically sorting emails in a variety of ways:

➢ Folders of your choosing.
➢ Copied or forwarded to another email address.
➢ Deleted or reject unwanted emails.
➢ Marking annoying senders as spam/junk, so they by-pass your inbox straight to the junk folder.
   o They don't have to by-pass your inbox if you so wish, they can remain in your inbox marked as spam.
   o When marked as spam, the email supplier or programs usually inserts the word SPAM in brackets at the front of the subject '[SPAM]'

The filters/rules you create, automatically searches all incoming mail and if they match one of your filters/rules, the action that you set is applied and either:

➢ move it to a designated folder.
➢ copy it to another folder.
➢ deletes it.
➢ forward a copy to another email address.
➢ or a combination of any of the above actions if you prefer.

Below are the steps in brief, followed by examples:

Step 1 – choose which parameter you want to search within the email; options are:

- ➢ Sender's name or email address.
- ➢ Subject line.
- ➢ Body containing specific words or phrases.

Step 2 – choose what keywords you want to search for within the email; options are:
- ➢ Various keywords exist or absent words (*does not contain….*).
- ➢ Exact match of your keywords or any of the words in your keyword selection if using more than one.
    - o E.g., spam email often deliberately misspells words to by-pass your filter, by swapping letter "O" for the number zero.

Step 3 – choose what action you wish to take with the email; options are:
- ➢ Delete it.
- ➢ Reject it. (Reject it sends an auto-reply back "this email was undeliverable").
- ➢ Move it to junk.
- ➢ Move or copy to another folder.
- ➢ Forward a copy to another email address.
- ➢ Leave it and flag it.
    - a. Flagging means the email will still appear in your inbox, but the subject usually changes to contain the word "[spam]" at the front of the subject.

You may have the option to run the new filter on your existing inbox emails.

Instructions – webmail accessed through your browser.
STEP-1 Log into your email and find your setting or options. This usually looks like one of the following four icons:

Fig-13.1

STEP-2 You should find located in the Settings an option that says 'filters'

GMAIL

Gmail has this icon Fig-13.2   , a menu drops down and select settings
Fig 13.3

‹ › ▦ ▾   ⚙

Display density

Configure inbox

Settings

Themes

Get add-ons

Send feedback

Help

Within settings, you will find Filters and Blocked Addresses and select Create A New Filter

Fig-13.4

Filters and Blocked Addresses

Fig-13.5

Create a new filter

The first window contains steps 1 & 2 – choosing what to search and which sections.

Example-1: I was receiving repeat emails about bit coins (a virtual currency) so I entered part of the words that were contained in the email "coins.ph". For good measure, I also entered into the email body parameter; *'Has the words'* "coins.ph", resulting in the filter searching all incoming email, where if either sender's name or the body of the email matches the filter. The email will be automatically dealt with below. See Fig 13.6 below for example.

Fig-13.6

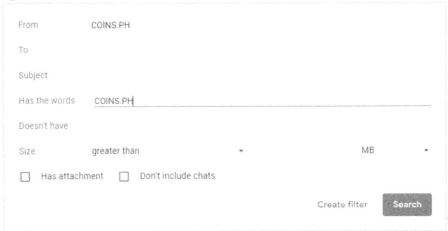

Once you enter some details, the Create filter button turns blue.
The second window contains step 3 – choosing what action to take with your email. Fig 13.7
E.g., in my example I just wanted to delete it.

Fig-13.7

←	When a message arrives that matches this search:
☐	Skip the Inbox (Archive it)
☐	Mark as read
☐	Star it
☐	Apply the label: Choose label... ▾
☐	Forward it add forwarding address
☑	Delete it
☐	Never send it to Spam
☐	Always mark it as important
☐	Never mark it as important
☐	Categorize as: Choose category... ▾
☐	Also apply filter to **0** matching conversations.
❷ Learn more	Create filter

But for many work items, I move certain emails to designated folders.
My wife's work receipts automatically forward a copy to my email for her accounts.

Example-2: You can set multiple parameters to search. In an attempt to get around the recipient setting filters/rules, senders would send their spam from a different email address each time. E.g., the junk mail is sent from joe1@eachbuyer.com then the junk mail sender will assume you have created a message filter/rule to filter out the junk mail, so the sender will alter their email so thus switching the senders email address e.g., joe2@eachbuyer.com. The words that are common to both spam emails is this case is, the name *'eachbuyer'*, instead of typing in the full email address to filter, enter just *'eachbuyer'* into multiple parameter sets so you have the greatest chance of catching all the spam from this individual/company. (See Figure 13.8 as an example).

Fig-13.8

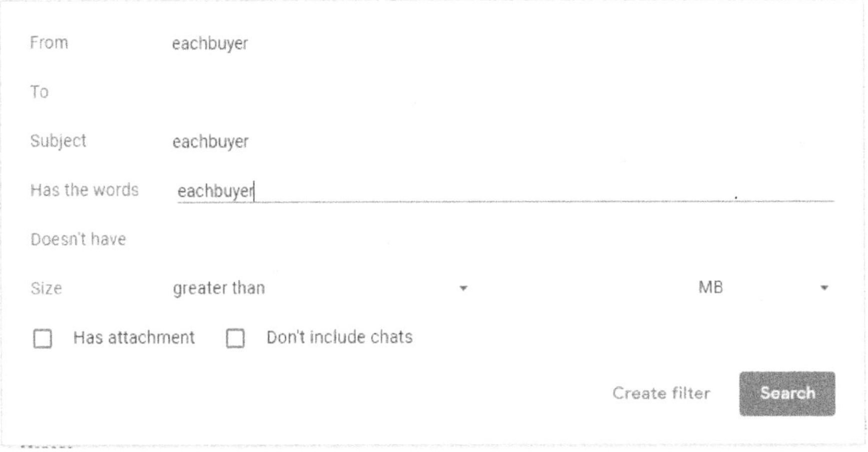

From	eachbuyer
To	
Subject	eachbuyer
Has the words	eachbuyer
Doesn't have	
Size	greater than ▾	MB ▾

☐ Has attachment   ☐ Don't include chats

Create filter   **Search**

Example-3: Fraudsters will often alter the spelling of certain words hoping to get around your filters. Say you are bombarded with emails about Viagra, the spammer will use more than spelling, e.g.: VIAGRA / with dashers V-I-A-G-R-A / or with spaces V I A G R A. To solve this problem, you create your message filter/rule with more than one word. (See Figure 13.9 as an example).

Fig-13.9

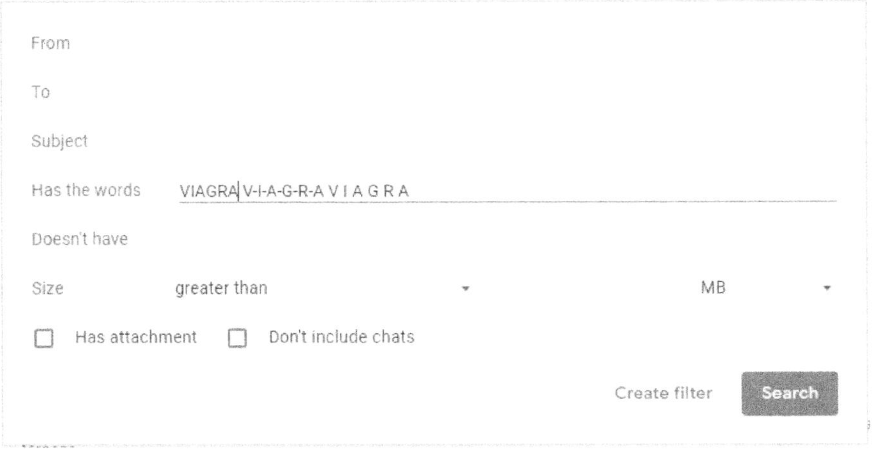

From	
To	
Subject	
Has the words	VIAGRA V-I-A-G-R-A V I A G R A
Doesn't have	
Size	greater than ▾	MB ▾

☐ Has attachment   ☐ Don't include chats

Create filter   **Search**

You can experiment and edit as much as you like.
Within other email providers, the filters will appear differently.

BLACKLISTING IS ALSO AN OPTION TO COMBAT SPAM

Blacklisting an email address only works if the fraudster uses the same sender's email.

Within Gmail/hotmail/outlook emails you have a button to report any email as spam. When you select and email and press this button, it moves that email to the spam folder. The gmail servers then learn that emails from this sender and of this type are spam and will increase the chances of future spam being identified; thus the more you idenify as spam yourself, the more it picks up automatically, the less you will get in future.

On some other email providers, the blacklist option is usually available on the right click when hovering over an email or when you select and email.

My best advice is to keep is to keep on top of spam mail by hitting the report spam mail button and using filters for persistent senders.

REMEMBER: For further assistance, contact your email provider. They will supply all the free help you require.

INSTRUCTION FOR EMAIL FILTERS/RULES WITHIN AN EMAIL PROGRAM

People who receive or send a lot of emails for work tend to use a program on their computer called 'an email client'. Some popular ones are: Windows live mail, Microsoft Outlook, Mozilla Thunderbird, Mailbird, Opera mail.

Email clients are great; you can organise your emails in far more detail – you can choose to store the emails on your PC or you can set your folders on the webmail and email client to mirror each other allowing you to use multiple devices to view and organise your emails.

Fig-13.10

Fig-13.11

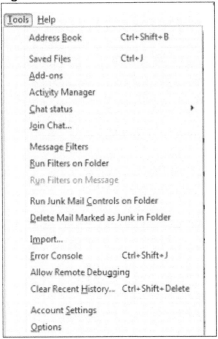

The principle is the same as creating filters in web-based emails;

Within an email program you have many more options. As well as searching by: From name, Subject or Email body, you can choose to show an alert for a particular email and apply rules. Example: I have old business email that will be deleted soon, but I want to warn colleagues. To assist I first create a filter/rule for any emails that are sent to my old email address, is moved into a folder of its own. When creating a filter/rule, one of the action options available is a *pop up alert*. So when I receive an email sent to my old email address, I receive an automatic pop-up in the middle of the screen alerting me to the issue.

With email programs such as Outlook, on step 3 of the filters/rules, you have many more action options.

TIPS
- ✓ Spam and junk filters are usually very good; hence I use this filter system for any persistent spam that always seems to get through.
- ✓ You can use the FILTER/RULE system for genuine reasons to help you organise emails automatically.
  - ○ If you receive a lot of routine emails for work that don't need to be read but just kept in case of a future problem, you can create a filter/rule that searches for a keyword that is unique to that sender, resulting in all the emails from that sender being moved and nicely organised into one separate folder.
  - ○ E.g.; say you are a hair hairdresser and purchase products online. You could create a rule containing the keyword *'hair'*, select it to be moved to a folder entitled *'hair folder'* or copy it to a second folder or forward it to your partner's email so they have a copy of your receipts for your bookkeeping.
- ✓ SPAM/JUNK SETTINGS I would not auto delete any spam, I suggest moving spam to your spam/junk folder so you can manually check that folder and not miss any important email.
  - ○ Sometimes genuine emails get picked up by the spam filter e.g., new ones or password reset emails, etc.
  - ○ You don't want such emails to be automatically deleted. You will want to be able to check yourself.
  - ○ Better that all spam goes to your spam/junk folder and review it once a month, or a time interval that suits you - especially if you are expecting an email that has not arrived e.g., password reset.
  - ○ There is usually an icon to mark a spam email in your inbox as spam/junk.
  - ○ There is usually an icon to mark a genuine email in your spam/junk folder as not spam/junk.
  - ○ If there is not an icon, I suggest right clicking to review your options - some email providers call it a blacklist & whitelist.
  - ○ After reviewing your spam/junk folder, you can usually empty it in one go.

14. SUMMARY ROUNDUP

MISCELLANEOUS

- ➢ If you have to allow access to a phone, computer or some online login, change the password to a temporary one and revert back afterwards.
- ➢ If your mobile/cell phone coverage goes dark – contact all your banks immediately.
- ➢ When in public, don't leave your phone on the table or bar, even for a second.
- ➢ Update your driving licence address as soon as you move.
- ➢ Don't keep valuables in your back pocket.
- ➢ Keep any external pocket zipped up.
- ➢ Carry a fake wallet with out-of-date bank card.
- ➢ Don't pat yourself down in a public area if there is a tannoy announcement.
- ➢ Wipe your hotel room key with a magnet.
- ➢ Don't use the *"please clean my room"* card.
- ➢ When you hand over your passport, double check the one returned is actually yours.
- ➢ If you lose sight of your bankcard, ensure the one-handed back is actually yours.
- ➢ Be wary of free Wi-Fi, don't access any sensitive items.
- ➢ Don't use public Wi-Fi for tasks such as banking, emails etc.
- ➢ Beware of anyone on dating websites asking for money, especially if you are in a virtual relationship and have never met; 99% will be a scam and you are being groomed.
- ➢ Don't let anyone use your bank account to put funds into and you draw them out or transfer onto a 3rd person after deducting a fee.
- ➢ You would not tell a complete stranger anything personal, do not do it online.
- ➢ Remember search YouTube for – *'amazing mind reader reveals his gifts'*.
- ➢ Always check the PIN pad terminal before paying by card.
- ➢ Always ask for receipt, even if you discard it later.
- ➢ Don't accept an overpayment and refund the balance. You may be assisting to commit fraud.

- ➤ Police or bank fraud teams will not involve the public with any investigation, it puts the public at risk, do not draw out money and hand anyone; a genuine police office or bank employee will not ask you to.
- ➤ Don't display your Wi-Fi code in the house.
- ➤ Unless you are in a shop, don't smell perfume samples from strangers.
- ➤ Verify any friend/family request for money.
- ➤ Always send £1/$1 to any new payee, and verify verbally, it was received.
- ➤ Larger transactions, verify the bank details verbally prior to setting it up.
- ➤ Never transfer money to a 'safe account'.

YOUR OWN EMAIL ADDRESS

- ➤ You may like to use your year of birth as 2 or 4 digits as part of your email address.
  - ○ E.g., bob70@ or bob1970@
- ➤ Probably, because the chosen email address is unavailable.
- ➤ However, if a fraudster sees happy birthday wishes on social media on any given day, they have now obtained your full DOB and are one step closer to gaining access to your bank or stealing your identity.
- ➤ For the same reason, don't wish somebody "happy 40th birthday" online.

FRAUDULENT EMAILS & TEXT

- ➤ Don't use tablets and phones to view suspicious emails.
- ➤ Use a browser on your device that has a mouse function.
- ➤ Be wary of emails. Hover over the *from address and* any links within the email to determine their authenticity.
- ➤ **Don't click on links in any text**.
- ➤ Don't click on links or attachment in any email you are unsure of.
- ➤ When reviewing emails or links, be wary of incorrect domain variations.
- ➤ Use email filters to help control the spam, or just to organise frequent email types.
- ➤ If your mobile/cell phone resets for no reason – contact all your banks immediately.

BROWSER AWARENESS & CLONED WEBSITES

➢ Install Trustee Rapport program to check you are using the correct bank websites.

➢ Use Favourites or Bookmarks to access banking websites or type the URL directly into the address bar.

➢ Don't use search engines for financial sites such as banking or other websites of sensitive nature.

➢ Watch for misspelt domains or hyphens (-) in domain names/web address.

SPOOF CALLS & GENUINE FRAUD CALLS FROM YOUR BANK

➢ Don't give out sensitive information: PIN/OTP/passwords etc.

➢ If in doubt, call your bank back USE THE PHONE NUMBER ON THE BANK OF THE CARD.

➢ Use a different phone. Call a friend first or wait an hour before using the phone.

➢ Be aware when receiving calls on a landline from a landline. Hanging up does not necessarily disconnect the call.

➢ Never press a number when asked to do so.

➢ Beware of aggressive and urgent calls.

BANKING & CARD USE

➢ Remove the PIN terminal from the cradle when paying in a shop.

➢ Cover your hand when entering your PIN.

➢ Never let the card out of your sight when using it.

➢ If you lose sight of your card, double check the one returned is yours.

➢ Be vigilant with ATMs in secluded places.

➢ Always sign your cards.

➢ Credit cards provide better protection online and with PayPal.

➢ Consider a separate bank accounts for spending and or continuous card authority transactions.

➢ Compartmentalise your banking so debit cards to important money are not at risk.

➢ Have accounts with different banks utilising the VISA and MASTERCARD NETWORK.

➢ If you have credit cards or prepaid cards, use both the VISA and MASTERCARD NETWORK.

MOBILE APPs
➢ Log out of Apps not in use to protect your personal details, especially when travelling or at large public events such as festivals, airports, bus & train terminals. (Also saves your battery).
➢ Disable Bluetooth and Wi-Fi when not using them in public areas & when travelling. (Also saves your battery).

STAYING SAFE ON Wi-Fi
➢ Mobile data is encrypted, public Wi-Fi is not.
➢ Install VPN on your device(s) for use on public Wi-Fi.

PASSWORDS & STRUCTURE IDEAS
➢ Consider creating a tier system to help you remember passwords.
➢ Always use a completely unique password for banking, PayPal, credit cards, emails, remote computer access & work stuff.
➢ Don't use pets, children or spouses as passwords.
➢ Consider the use of a password manager.
➢ Keep a short auto-log off period.
➢ Don't use the password manager for banking or emails.

ROUTER & HOME NETWORK
➢ Free help available from your internet provider.
➢ Change the default router admin password.
➢ Change the default Wi-Fi password.
➢ Turn off the router when away on holiday, unless you require remote access to your computer or smart heating to control the heating when you are on your way home.
➢ Turn off Wi-Fi when away on holiday if you are leaving your router on.
➢ Ensure your SSID (Wi-Fi name) does not identify you personally.
➢ Set up the guest Wi-Fi network for visitors.
➢ Change the guest Wi-Fi password regularly.
➢ Consider MAC address filtering.
➢ Consider turning off SSID broadcast. If any device stops working e.g., TV box, you can turn SSID broadcast back on.
➢ Consider a cable connection for static devices such as TV boxes.
➢ Used timed access for workplace; switch on one hour before and off one hour after; allows for occasional early starters or late finishers.

- ➤ Always change your Wi-Fi password when members of staff leave <u>for any reason</u>.

DOMAIN NAMES
- ➤ Free help available from domain companies.
- ➤ Consider buying a domain name.
- ➤ You can use just mail forwarding to a free mailbox e.g., Gmail or Hotmail etc. and create as many aliases as you like.
- ➤ You can pay a little more for email hosting so you can send mail from your domain and create unlimited email addresses for your personal/business use.

PayPal
- ➤ If your PayPal is compromised – do not delete the account; change the password, cancel all linked cards in your PayPal wallet, create a new email, add it, make it the primary email and remove the old email.
- ➤ Create multiple PayPal accounts with multiple email addresses, either with a domain name or free email accounts.
- ➤ Register only one card per PayPal account.
- ➤ Only register credit cards where possible.

REDUCING SPAM EMAIL & AUTO-ORGANISATION
- ➤ Free help available from your internet provider.
- ➤ Create filters/rules to help auto-organise your incoming mail.
- ➤ Create filters/rules to help prevent unwanted mail from ever being received.

<u>REMEMBER THE ABC RULE</u>
- A. ASSUME NO ONE IS GENUINE
- B. BELIEVE NOTHING YOU HEAR
- C. CHALLENGE EVERYTHING
- D. DON'T RETURN ANY PHONE CALLS USING NUMBERS SUPPLIED BY THE FRAUDSTER
- E. TAKE 5 (5mins) - THINK

I hope you have at least found some of these things useful. I developed my ideas and protocols by observing people and hearing their stories from around the world over the last 30-years. Many of these tactics are simple and straightforward; we just have to remember to act on them. I wish you well in living a more secure life.

FURTHER RESOURCES

I created a website to publish scams I am aware of and hopefully update the website with future scams. The book will remain the most informative way of implementing my protocols and advice.

There is also a PDF download available of my proposed banking structure and how to compartmentalise your banking.

Please visit my website for new scams in the future and the PDF download. I am sure more content will be available in the future.

www.beatthefraudster.com

ACKNOWLEDGEMENTS

I would like to thank the following people for their assistance & comments on the book before publishing:

- ➤ DS Cananur (Kent Police Fraud Specialist & Hunter on the Channel 4 programme *'Hunted'* and BBC show *'For Love or Money'*).
- ➤ DCI Cavin (Devon & Cornwall Police; Head of a Serious and Organised Crime Branch including Fraud and Cyber units).
- ➤ Paul Lewis (Journalist & BBC Radio 4 presenter of the MoneyBox programme).
- ➤ Laura Rimmer and her team for assisting in getting this book to market.

Printed in Great Britain
by Amazon